The Decline of the Hollywood Empire

The Decline of the Hollywood Empire

Hervé Fischer

Translated by Rhonda Mullins

Talonbooks
Vancouver

Copyright © 2004 VLB Éditeur
Translation copyright © 2006 Rhonda Mullins

Talonbooks
P.O. Box 2076, Vancouver, British Columbia, Canada V6B 3S3
www.talonbooks.com

Typeset in Scala and ScalaSans and printed and bound in Canada.

First Printing: 2006

The publisher gratefully acknowledges the financial support of the Canada
Council for the Arts; the Government of Canada through the Book
Publishing Industry Development Program; and the Province of British
Columbia through the British Columbia Arts Council for our publishing
activities.

Le déclin de l'empire hollywoodien by Hervé Fischer was first published in
French in 2004 by VLB Éditeur in Montreal. Financial support for this
translation provided by the Canada Council for the Arts and the
Department of Canadian Heritage through the Book Publishing Industry
Development Program.

Library and Archives Canada Cataloguing in Publication

Fischer, Hervé, 1941–
    The decline of the Hollywood empire / Hervé Fischer ; translated by
Rhonda Mullins.

Translation of: Le déclin de l'empire hollywoodien.
Includes bibliographical references.
ISBN 0-88922-545-1

    1. Motion picture industry—California. 2. Hollywood (Los Angeles,
Calif.). 3. Independent filmmakers. I. Mullins, Rhonda, 1966– II. Title.

PN1993.5.U65F5613 2006   338.4'7791430979494   C2006-904407-4

ISBN-10: 0-88922-545-1
ISBN-13: 978-0-88922-545-9

CONTENTS

LIST OF ACRONYMS

ACTRA	Alliance of Canadian Cinema, Television and Radio Artists
ADN	Agence européenne pour le développement du cinéma numérique (European Agency for the Development of Digital Film)
ALPA	Association de lutte contre le piratage audiovisuel (Association for the Fight Against Audiovisual Piracy)
CNA	Cinéma numérique ambulant (Travelling Digital Cinema)
CNC	Centre national de la cinématographie (National Film Centre)
DCEN	D-Cinema Europa Network
EDCF	European Digital Cinema Forum
EIC	Entertainment Industry Coalition for Free Trade
ESA	European Space Agency
GATT	General Agreement on Tariffs and Trade
GFC	General Film Company
ICAIC	Instituto Cubano del Arte e Industria Cinematográficos (Cuban Institute for Film Arts and Industry)

I-DIFF	International Digital Film Forum
ILM	Industrial Light and Magic (a Lucasfilm company)
INCAA	Instituto Nacional de Cine y Artes Audiovisuales (National Institute of Film and Audiovisual Arts – Argentina)
MGM	Metro-Goldwyn-Mayer
MPA	Motion Picture Association
MPAA	Motion Picture Association of America
MPEA	Motion Picture Export Association
MPPA	Motion Picture Producers Association
MPPC	Motion Picture Patents Company
NATO	National Association of Theater Owners
NFB	National Film Board of Canada
SODEC	Société de développement des entreprises culturelles (Society for the Development of Cultural Enterprises – Quebec)
UA	United Artists
UIP	United International Pictures
WTO	World Trade Organization

Digital cinema is inevitable, so we might as well get on with it.
George Lucas

ALL EMPIRES MUST FALL

Empires are an endless source of fascination. At certain moments in time, they spur major changes around the world, and generally have larger-than-life figures at their source. They make their mark by imposing the law of the jungle and destroying much along the way. The empire I'm referring to here is not the empire of Alexander the Great or the Roman Empire, but the Hollywood empire, a glorious industry, symbol of American imperialism.

Over the years, Hollywood has designed and instituted a complex and extraordinarily rational method of operating—the studio system—in order to build and control its empire. Its power derives from a dynamic organization consistent down to the last detail, without which its sweeping worldwide success would not have been possible. Dissecting a model of such rare ingenuity is a fascinating task. But it is even more interesting to do so just as a foreign body, in the form of digital technology, is looming, with the capacity to destroy, in just a few short years, a system that has been skilfully built up over a century. And that's precisely what's going to happen.

But first, we must render unto Caesar. Hollywood has built a powerful global industry that has produced not just the flops that stream from its studios, but masterpieces as well.

Initial homage paid, and with the inevitable decline of this empire on the horizon, there is a distinction to be made between the talent of Hollywood film artists and the talent of the financial moguls who still reign over the empire, unaware that it is giving way from underneath their gilded chairs. Delivering a eulogy prematurely may seem offensive, but the true offence lies in the Hollywood cartel's cynical exercise of its hegemony around the world, as it exploits film with no regard for its creative power or for cultural diversity.

With Hollywood's inevitable collapse, we may see the first signs of the crumbling of American imperialism on the horizon. It's hardly surprising that a country would impose its cultural industries on us when the military budget of that country is $400 billion annually, or more than $1 billion a day, exceeding the 20 next-largest military budgets combined, and when its financial power means that it can arbitrarily impose *Pax Americana*, whether through force or by working behind the scenes. Grandeur and decadence characterize this story. With Hollywood's decline, we may be able to achieve (has such a world ever existed but in our dreams) a balance between different flavours, styles, and cultures that belong to us all.

It's hard not to criticize the imperialism of an entertainment industry created through in-your-face marketing that tries to steamroll the planet, destroying art and freedom in film, an industry that generates wealth by impoverishing the art form and casually killing off independent theatres.

But to every empire there is a season, fortunately. The advent of digital cinema—not only in production and post-production, but also and especially in distribution—is already shaking the foundations of this vast empire, which, it turns out, is as fragile as it is arrogant. Digital technology is going to give film a second wind. It will be the Hollywood empire's Trojan horse.

There are two Americas: the creative one that we love and want to see revived, and the imperialist one we love less. The Hollywood empire has been built with the steady support of successive governments, both Democratic and Republican. But the spirit of this book is not anti-American. It is dedicated to Max, my American grandson. And it is dedicated to Québecois filmmaker Denys Arcand, in particular for two of his films: *The Decline of the American Empire* and *The Barbarian Invasions*, which ironically won him an Oscar at the temple of Hollywood. He accepted it close-mouthed, looking somewhat bemused.

Revolutions in Film

Cinema was not always commercially driven with the mass-market blockbusters that Hollywood regularly foists upon us in the darkened movie theatres of the world. Its history has been punctuated with memorable auteur films that have explored every creative avenue available. Remembering the origins of cinema helps us better understand the seriousness of the decline of Hollywood and of those who are subject to the system. Film was actually born of a boldness and artistry that the current lords of the manor now devote solely to the quest for profit.

Hollywood's history is intertwined with a series of technological inventions: photography, the perforated film strip and cameras that capture 24 frames per second, the projector, sound, colour, and the move from silver emulsion film to digital and computer-generated images.

Astonishingly, the only thing that hasn't evolved in Hollywood in the past hundred years is its means of distribution, which is still based on the labour-intensive and ruinously expensive process of making hundreds of prints and delivering heavy reels of film to every single theatre. Digital distribution will end this archaic system of distribution and hasten the decline of the Hollywood empire: two giant steps forward for film in one fell swoop!

But before delving into this second technological revolution in film, we first need to look at the major stages of the first revolution that led up to it: the revolution in production and projection.

From Georges Méliès to George Lucas: it's been quite a ride! A century of incredible innovation in film, initiated by a Parisian alchemist of celluloid and purveyor of travelling screenings, who is resurrected today on-screen by a Californian emperor of the digital world. Both filmmakers tell somewhat simplistic, sentimental stories. Lucas's made-in-Hollywood special effects have nothing on those of Méliès's short, funny, black-and-white photoplays. And both filmmakers love the sky, the moon, the sun, and the stars. So ends the first era in the technological epic of film.

Georges Méliès, born into a family of shoemakers, had the gift of being able to cobble together not only leather-working machines, but also puppet theatres, which he made while tucked away in his attic. Méliès studied painting with Gustave Moreau and learned sleight-of-hand from the famous London illusionist David Devant. He then discovered the appropriately named Lumière brothers' world of film and redirected his talents to shooting and editing movies. He had the same uncanny ability with light and form that his family had with leather. He could make an aquarium pass for an ocean. He was a pioneer and a genius. When Jean-Christophe Averty tried to recreate Méliès's special effects in his film *Méliès, le magicien de Montreuil-sous-Bois*, he had a great deal of difficulty, even though he was working a half-century later.

The history of cinema started with puppets and Chinese shadow plays, followed by the magic lantern. Along with sleight-of-hand, celluloid, and silver emulsion film, CinemaScope took hold. Silent films became talkies. Film went colour. Unfortunately, it also went Hollywood. But that's not where the story ends, because now film is going to go digital, and digital technology is ideally suited to the magic lantern of the imagination, as Marshall McLuhan liked to call film. The digital age of film has three distinct chronological stages: first, scarce and expensive special effects, then completely digital productions, and finally, distribution, which is in the process of becoming entirely digital as well. We are on the verge of the rise of totally digital film. Soon the 35 mm celluloid reels around which the Hollywood empire is wound will be used to store films in the vaults of cinematheques and nothing more.

Ironically, film has come full circle. Digital technology's rise has brought about a return to special effects and the unreality that was at the origins of the art form. Think back to the Lumière brothers' famous locomotive hurtling into the station at La Ciotat in December 1895 and seeming to jump off the screen into the frightened audience at the Grand Café de Lyon!

Méliès the magician preferred the technological conjuring film made possible. He despised Charlie Chaplin (who nonetheless admired him), because according to Méliès, what Chaplin was doing was clowning on screen and not making film. He refused to shoot on location and criticized film for having abandoned its capacity for illusion by becoming filmed theatre with storybook narratives unfolding on realistic sets with no flights of fancy. The darkened theatres of the 20th century plunged further and further into visual and psychological realism, some might even say miserabilism, which Méliès anticipated and criticized. But today's growing expertise with computer-generated images and animation software is releasing naturalism's grip over creativity in film, which the genre slavishly adopted from photography.

Montreal, the midpoint between Montreuil and Los Angeles, where Léo-Ernest Ouimet opened his first Ouimetoscope in 1906, has been a site for the revival of film. For Expo 67, Canada's National Film Board (NFB), already famous for its animation studio created in 1942 under the influence of Norman McLaren and others, stretched film to the largest format seen to that point—the precursor to IMAX—projecting on a screen that was seven storeys high. And at the beginning of the 1980s, Montreal once again made film history. Eschewing the camera and celluloid in favour of the computer and magnetic tape, abandoning analogue for algorithms, film veered off radically and cast off the shackles of realism. Ironically, digital technology has helped film return to its roots. Daniel Langlois, Pierre Lachapelle, Pierre Robidoux, and Denis Bergeron, four young students trained by Nadia and Daniel Thalmann, a Swiss couple who worked at the Université de Montréal for a time, set about producing the first 3D film created entirely on a computer, *Tony de Peltrie*. Working nights, when it was easier to get access to the university's mainframe, they told the story of an aging pianist who dreams of a youth filled with worldly hopes and female conquests; for the first time, filmmakers used polygons and pixels to depict not only mass and movement, but also, and most significantly, facial expressions.

A short while later, Daniel Langlois founded Montreal-based Softimage, and Steven Spielberg used the company's software to create and animate the dinosaurs in *Jurassic Park* (1993), blazing the trail for the California filmmakers who created *Twister, Titanic, The Matrix, Men in Black, The Mask,* and others.

During the same period, beginning in 1982, Walt Disney Studios began producing computer animation and used computer-generated images in the making of *Tron*, directed by Steven Lisberger. At the same time, George Lucas's Lucas Computer Graphics Division, which also created movie special effects, hired John Lasseter. The company was bought out shortly afterwards by Apple co-founder Steve Jobs and rebaptized Pixar, but before the change of ownership Lasseter produced his first masterpieces of computer animation: *Luxo Jr.* (1986), *Red's Dream* (1987), Oscar-winner *Tin Toy* (1988), and then *Toy Story* in 1995, the first feature animation film produced entirely using digital technology, followed by *Toy Story 2* in 1997. George Lucas then founded Industrial Light and Magic (ILM), a division of Lucas Digital. Walt Disney distributed all of these digital animation films, and as a result they gained wide visibility, as did the special effects in *Star Wars*. But the first digital short film was nonetheless *Tony de Peltrie*, produced in Montreal in 1985, and it carries even greater historical weight given that it was based on an actual screenplay.

The Wachowski brothers' *Matrix*, with its visual trickery and uncertainty-inducing blend of the virtual and the real, will also go down in the history of this return to the original, fantastical spirit of film. *The Matrix* does not simply use digital technology; it presents a digital world that enslaves humans by neurocognitively simulating reality, using the story-telling technique of *mise en abyme*. *The Matrix* is reminiscent of Plato's allegory of the cave, setting the illusions of our senses and the realities of our mind in opposition. But the film comes down in favour of artists and poets, unlike Plato, who called them liars unworthy of the Republic. In today's screen society, pinching yourself is not sufficient to distinguish between analogue and digital, between waking and dreaming, between the natural and the virtual, to be sure of which is more real! Realism is giving way under the weight of the digital realm.

There is a move away from traditional realist film—Soviet realism of the 1920s, Italian neorealism of 1942 to 1951, the New Wave ushered in with the *Cahiers du cinema* in 1959, and cinéma vérité of the 1960s. Contemporary creativity in film can reconnect with the imaginative freedom and unfettered fantasy of its beginnings, when Méliès, the alchemist of light, as Charlie Chaplin called him, used his talents to bring us the unreal.

But what does the freedom that computer-generated images allow film once again really cultivate? Have the constraints of naturalist realism, gigantic reconstructions of urban settings and battlefields, with their staggering budgets, become a thing of the past now that actors can be superimposed on virtual sets? Is that what the Hollywood majors, the Californian mammoths of the infamous Motion Picture Association of America (MPAA), have in store for us?

Freed from social and psychological realism, we find ourselves plunged in the mediocre commercial realism of a mass entertainment industry. Because under Hollywood's leadership, film has become an oppressive industry, entirely dependent on the logic of accounting. In the end, reduced to an industry of capturing markets, the art of film is subject to a realism that is worse than the naturalism that came before it: the realism of money. This unfortunate era of film should be called business realism.

We are witnessing the planet-wide success of a commercial, formulaic cinema, in which the scripts, the casting, and the sets are based on short-sighted market analyses rather than on the vision of filmmakers. Movies contain just the right doses of love, sex, violence, evil, good, virtue, and political ideology to hopefully guarantee profits, inevitably imposing formulas that producers and directors, prisoners of the Hollywood system, must follow.

So much money is now invested in the film industry that commercially and politically it has to be global. In just one century, Hollywood has strayed very far indeed from the vision of Méliès.

And why not? What about creativity? What about auteur films, repertory theatres, alternative or national cinema? What about activist filmmaking with a social purpose? What about the cultural diversity of film? Creative freedom even for Hollywood filmmakers? The freedom to see other forms of film? It has all been slowly disappearing.

The irony is that film has never had so much money ... and so little creative freedom. Too much money, it turns out, can kill film just as sure as not enough. And more insidiously, perhaps.

And yet, as destiny would have it, the glorious name "Hollywood" ends with a *d*, harbinger of the birth of d-cinema, digital cinema, which will mark the end of the Hollywood empire. The behemoths of Hollywood celluloid will soon be an endangered species.

At the beginning of the 21st century, now that American cultural, commercial, and military imperialism has reached the heights it has under the administration of George W. Bush, when widespread patriotism and fundamentalism are peddled alongside film, with no attempt to hide the long-standing collusion between the Pentagon, the White House, and Hollywood, it's time for digital technology to open up the lateral fields of vision they have set as off-limits. In McLuhan's global village, which is ruled by an imperial power that McLuhan did not anticipate, it would be nice if village cultures, those of Denys Arcand's barbarians, had as much, if not more, right to exist as the great games of the imperial circus that the Hollywood machine has been boring us with for so long.

Quiet on the set! Action! The 35 mm reels unwind; and so does the history of film, intertwined with 35 mm technology. But now, history is starting to unwind faster! And digital technology is a revolution in the making.

To outlive itself, Hollywood needs to adapt and renew its imperialism by adopting digital distribution, something that is virtually unthinkable. This new method of distribution will erode the foundations of Hollywood's control, just when the empire is financially vulnerable. Like the face of an aging Tony de Peltrie, the symbolic sign in the fabled hills is already pixelizing and fading away.

The decline of the Hollywood empire will take more than just a few weeks: it won't come about *the day after tomorrow*, as in Roland Emmerich's $125 million picture about a sudden ice age in New York. The empire will fight back, pick itself back up, and maybe even give us a swan song before falling. But it *will* fall. Its decline may take a decade. The story of the Tower of Babel will come true once more, for the general good. Film will come back multilingual and multicultural, with more and different ideas from all quarters, and less money.

Of course, some of the blockbusters that have unwound from chrome cases on Technicolor film, saturated in candy colours, are worthy of our affection, and one day, when we are able to see something new, to see other styles of movies from other parts of the world, we may even indulge in a little nostalgia, like the nostalgia of Westerns. The digital revolution tolls the bell for the empire, but it heralds newfound freedom for film, more in keeping with its true nature and social purpose, closer to Giuseppe Tornatore's *Cinema Paradiso* and his unforgettable projectionist Philippe Noiret, so far from the Hollywood stereotype!

Holly Wood, Holy Wood

At the beginning of the 20th century, the Hollywood Hills, if we are to believe the name, were supposedly covered with holly. We can now take away an *l* from the name, because the holly shrubs with their thorny leaves have made way for the myth of a truly sacred wood: Holy Wood. The first hills that were emblems of a new empire witnessed the construction of the temples of American film and the renowned star system. Holy Holly Wood! The legend of the origins that celebrates this modern-day Rome of American film also includes several hills, among them the famous Beverly Hills. But today, the hallowed ground is covered with studios and CEO offices, having been transformed into a factory for American dreams.

Unlike the Roman Empire, no she-wolf figures in the beginnings of Hollywood. In 1886, there was a single ranch, then a village, which became part of Los Angeles in 1903, with a mix of social classes that would be unthinkable today among Hollywood's rich and powerful. Film's Romulus was Francis Boggs of the Selig Polyscope Company, who arrived from Chicago in 1907 looking for sunny locations for his film *Monte Cristo*. In 1909, he opened a first studio in the city, where he would shoot *The Heart of a Race Tout*. He was murdered shortly thereafter. But others came in turn, escaping the commercial litigation of Edison, who ruled the

East Coast and New York: D. W. Griffith of Biograph came, as did Thomas Ince of the New York Picture Company to film his first Westerns, Cecil B. DeMille came to make *The Squaw Man*, followed by New York's Vitagraph, Lubin Studios, Carl Laemmle of the Universal Film Manufacturing Company, Fox, Triangle, and Warner. It was 1918 and Hollywood's fate was sealed. These dynamic entrepreneurs started to attract foreign émigré filmmakers and took control of distribution as well as production. The Second World War that was to ravage Europe gave Hollywood free rein to consolidate its empire.

Malevolence, American-style

Perforated strips of celluloid unwind from 35 mm reels like the *Via Romana* in the U.S., which in 1930 already had some 15,000 theatres; worldwide, there were around 50,000. Hollywood producers were already organizing to occupy the market and erect barriers to entry, even locking out their American competitors who had failed to join their conglomerate. In 1912, Hollywood producers decided to initiate proceedings with the U.S. Department of Justice against Edison's Motion Picture Patents Company (MPPC) and the General Film Company (GFC) for monopoly abuse and illegal anti-competitive agreements using the Sherman Antitrust Act of 1888, an antiquated law that was not designed for these types of charges. In 1915 and 1917 respectively, the federal government dissolved the GFC and the MPPC, declaring their practices illegal.

These companies would, however, try to carry on, and in 1927 the Famous Players–Lasky Corporation was convicted. The majors, the big five, as they were already called, were buying up theatre chains and trying to control the other exhibition networks by imposing second-rate movies tied to the right to premiere hit films. The Hollywood machine had become so abusive again that the other American production and distribution companies once more reacted decisively.

In 1940, in the face of continued illegal activity, the federal government, which had relaunched suits against the majors, imposed a consent decree on the studios, forcing them to agree to limit these practices. Once the Second World War ended, the U.S. Department of Justice again initiated legal proceedings in *U.S. v. Paramount et al.*, also known as the New York Equity Suit, upheld in the Supreme Court in 1948, trying to force Paramount and the majors yet again to limit their monopoly practices. However, the new ruling did not require that the majors immediately relinquish ownership of their powerful network of theatres (which constituted vertical concentration) on account of the difficulties they professed to be having in shoring up their industry against the erosion of their overseas network of theatres on the heels of the Second World War and dealing with burgeoning competition from television. It took Paramount until 1951 to divest itself of its chain of theatres, United Paramount Theaters, which the ABC television network bought up in 1953—showing that this typically American will to power was already widespread, and that the legislator, supposedly concerned about commercial equilibrium, could do no better than to shift the problem, perceived as a virtue, from capitalist hand to capitalist hand, each one more ruthless than the last. This dream of ultimate power is still alive and well in the U.S.: witness the failed battle against Microsoft, the various forms of accounting fraud, and the arrogant politics of President George W. Bush himself, a two-bit Caesar for the 21st century. American malevolence has spread like a virus, wreaking havoc both domestically and internationally. America's very spirit is contaminated.

The New York Equity Suit resulted in the birth of a host of subcontracting companies that revolve around the majors. The result is what you could call the Hollywood oligopoly: a conglomerate of companies at all levels of production and distribution that occupy every possible niche.

Back then, the Paramount ruling prevented the majors from acquiring TV networks, but even this limitation no longer exists.

The United States was the majors' testing ground for organizing a cartel and eliminating their competition, which they then did systematically in foreign markets. And with few exceptions, the proliferation of global and bilateral free trade agreements and the triumph of ultraliberalism have allowed them to exercise their power worldwide with significantly fewer legal restrictions than in their own country. The virtues of competition that are held up domestically do not seem to apply to the rest of the world. In fact, the American government has a long history of helping the majors overcome legal obstacles and political resistance around the world.

The Big Seven

This culture of capitalist hegemony is clearly congenital to Hollywood. The majors have it in their blood, and the MPAA is the lynchpin of the control machine. The MPAA represents the major producers, or the big seven: Walt Disney/Buena Vista, Sony Columbia Tristar, Metro-Goldwyn-Mayer (MGM), Paramount Pictures Entertainment, Twentieth Century Fox Film Corporation, Universal Studios, and Warner Bros. Steven Spielberg's DreamWorks is a contender for the eighth spot. And with the recent sale of MGM to Sony, the big seven have a chance to further consolidate their power. Plus, they control a hundred or more supposedly "independent" production and distribution companies, called the indies to distinguish them from the majors. Through the indies, the majors can occupy every niche, potentially even local and alternative networks for art, experimental, and low-budget film.

It's not surprising that behind the curtain are the major communications multinationals, large international empires that hold financial stakes in the big seven. AOL/Time Warner owns Warner Brothers Pictures, and Turner Broadcasting bought "independents" such as New Line Cinema and Castle Rock Entertainment in the 1990s. In 1989, Sony acquired Columbia Pictures Entertainment, with its two production companies (Columbia Pictures and Tristar Pictures), two TV companies (Columbia Pictures Television and Merv Griffin Enterprises), and the Loews film distribution chain. In 1993 Walt Disney/Buena Vista bought the largest independent distribution company in existence, Miramax Films, in which it retains a stake. Viacom, a major television and cable conglomerate, bought Paramount, the Blockbuster video and DVD chain in 1993, and the CBS television network in 2000. Like other conglomerates, Viacom also heads up a smaller-budget art and experimental film company, Paramount Classics. News Corp, the Australian media giant controlled by Rupert Murdoch, acquired Fox in 1985, which has since become the Twentieth Century Fox Film Corporation. Of course, News Corp controls countless other communication companies around the world, including television networks, magazines, and newspapers. Universal Studios and NBC are both property of General Electric. The French company Vivendi took up the charge and in 2000 bought Universal Studios. It has since had to relinquish the company, which of course makes no difference to movie audiences. These conglomerates are playing a game of Monopoly: the law of capitalist control is the constant while players exchange cards. Film has become a global industry, controlled by major financial holding companies that do not necessarily have any particular expertise in media and that buy up successful independents to ensure that they maintain absolute control of the board.

A Distribution Industry

When we think Hollywood, we tend to think production, but it has a powerful distribution industry as well. The set-up is simple: to produce movies profitably, you need to be able to distribute everywhere. Whoever owns the distribution network has the key to the whole building, so long as there are films to distribute. Members of this increasingly powerful and complex conglomerate are completely interdependent.

According to statistics provided by the North American Industry Classification System, the county of Los Angeles alone plays host to close to half of all American film and DVD distribution companies and workers.

Marketing and promotional budgets for A-movies are as staggering as those for the productions themselves!

Since former actor Ronald Reagan became president, the federal government has been much more tolerant of the lax interpretation of the antitrust law of 1948, encouraging a return to vertical integration of distribution networks and production companies into vast conglomerates, which are incidentally becoming less transparent by virtue of their financial complexity and the fact that they operate transnationally.

In 2000, with the release of 170 pictures, the ten major distributors, Buena Vista, Universal, Warner Bros, Twentieth Century Fox, Paramount, DreamWorks, Sony, Miramax (Disney), New Line (Warner), and USA Films earned more than $7 billion domestically (of which Buena Vista and Universal alone earned more than $2 billion), representing an average box-office take of $41.7 million per picture.[1]

Jeremy Rifkin, media-friendly guru of cultural capitalism, refers to the exemplary case of Hollywood, pointing to an analysis performed by two film industry specialists, Asu Aksoy and Kevin Robins, who maintain that the movement to organization in networks is the key to cinema's commercial success: "By holding on to their power as national and international distribution networks, the majors were able to use their financial muscle to dominate the film business and to squeeze or to use the independent production companies."[2] Of course, just as the entire automotive industry depends on reseller networks, Hollywood quickly understood that it had to control reliable distribution networks. But in the American auto industry, there are no manufacturing cartels, and vendors of competing makes of cars can do business in the same town, whereas Hollywood has ensured that it has as much control as is possible over major theatres across the country.

The most common system of operating involves sharing revenue between theatre owners and distributors who receive 60% of the box office the first week, 50% the second week, and 40% the following weeks. In the U.S. itself, the big seven control the large multiplexes that are strategically located around major urban centres. Multiplexes premiere major films and their box-office revenues account for 80% of the total box office for American theatres. B-movies and experimental or art films distributed by Universal, Columbia, or United Artists (UA) are shown in more marginal theatres. If you look at the true independents—which should actually be called outsiders rather than indies—their theatres represent only 2.5% of total screens, and auteur films only 5% of box-office revenues.

And, of course, independent producers do not have a distribution network and have to rely on major networks. Even a filmmaker as prominent as Steven Spielberg appeared on United International Pictures' (UIP) website expressing his gratitude that UIP has distributed almost all of his movies around the world and almost everything Amblin has produced over the years, praising their unparalleled devotion and conscientiousness. He saluted all those who had worked so hard in large and small markets, distributing his features, short films, blockbusters, and more sensitive films. And Peter Howitt and Andrés V. Gómez added their photo to the chorus of praise on the UIP website—praise that Woody Allen, Michael Moore, Gus van Sant (whose film *Elephant* won the Golden Palm at the Cannes Film Festival in 2003, but that was not widely distributed and therefore unjustly forgotten), Larry Clark, Amos Kollek, Todd Solondz, and Jim Jarmusch, all Hollywood outsiders marginalized by distribution networks, are not prepared to offer, unless one day they are lured by the Hollywood siren!

Vertical and Horizontal Concentration of Ownership

The American strategy of concentration in ownership has never flagged. In the early days of film, one of its American inventors, Thomas Edison, engaged in a long legal battle to win recognition of the monopoly of his patent (which was hotly contested at the time, Edison being only one among many inventors, such as the Lumière brothers), and as a result he imposed a licence fee on American theatres for the exhibition of movies.

Madeleine Malthête-Méliès, granddaughter of Georges Méliès, discusses this in the inspiring 1985 book she dedicated to Méliès the magician, in which she describes the negotiations that ended in the creation of the MPAA's predecessor: "On December 18, 1908, the largest trust yet was formed. It included Edison, Biograph, Vitagraph, Lubin, Selig, Essanay, Kalem, Pathé, and Gaston Méliès (in the name of Star-Film and the Méliès Manufacturing Company). The Motion Picture Patents Company (MPPC) was born!"[3]

The Motion Picture Producers Association (MPPA) would carry the torch after the First World War and in 1922 would form an association with distributors, the Motion Picture Producers and Distributors Association.

The problem of concentration among production companies dates back even earlier than this, with the birth of France's film editors association, the Chambre syndicale des éditeurs de films, in 1900, with Georges Méliès at the helm. His granddaughter recalls the motives behind its creation, as recounted by its founders: "Certain large production houses were trying to use their enormous capital to crush others, and we thought it was a good idea to form a group to defend our corporate interests."[4]

Since its beginnings, film has sought to move beyond art and into industry, a power grab, where commercial logic prevails over artistic considerations, marginalizing auteur films like those that Méliès and his cohorts created. Méliès was very much a victim of this commercial mentality. He was ruined and ended his professional life as a candy merchant in the Montparnasse train station concourse in 1923. In rage and despair, he even burned his films and the archives he kept at his house in Montreuil. Henri Langlois and Georges Franju, creators of the Cinémathèque française, later had to go to great lengths to find and save prints of his films, most of which were scratched and incomplete. The fate of film was sealed early on, and Hollywood's hegemony came to define how the rest of the story would unfold.

But movie production is only one aspect of the power of major producers, who, apart from movie box-office receipts, exploit a full range of merchandise (gadgets, action figures, toys, food and clothing tie-ins, and hit soundtracks), as well as videos and DVDs. And because they are part of powerful media multinationals, producers also control TV networks, magazine and newspaper groups, internet networks, and more, giving them plenty of opportunity for cross-promotion. They also operate powerful conglomerates that vertically integrate production and distribution—the content and the pipes—and offer promotional opportunities across a full spectrum of sister companies.

Small, so-called independent companies, the indies, do not appear to work directly for the big seven, but in fact they orbit Hollywood like satellites. The illusion of their independence has made it possible for specialists in the field to believe there is a true separation between the majors and the independents. But it's all a smokescreen. In reality, the indies are completely dependent on distribution networks, or on films that depend on distribution networks. They offer the big seven the advantage of occupying every niche and eliminating competition from outside of the cartel. The indies remain within the sphere of influence of the big seven and even act as a pool of talent and expertise that the majors can draw from.

The indies include producers of art and experimental film, documentaries, and of course also porn, a particularly profitable type of venture, centred mainly in the San Fernando valley.

Diversity in American independent film does exist, attempting to connect with audiences in search of auteur films. But in the U.S., as in other countries, it will take the fall of the Hollywood empire for creative films that reflect our diversity to move out of the shadows and take their rightful place in American culture.

1. The Hollywood Reporter, *Film 500*.

2. Jeremy Rifkin, "Hollywood for the 21st Century: Global Competition for Critical Mass in Image Markets," *Cambridge Journal of Economics* 16, no. 16 (March 1992): 9.

3. Madeleine Malthête-Méliès, *Méliès l'enchanteur* (Paris: Hachette, 1973), 321.

4. Ibid., 232.

Holly World

Having seen how Hollywood jockeyed for power in the U.S., we can now move on to the big seven's takeover of the rest of the planet and how it uses most of its resources to sustain its lifestyle, like a lord over his lands of years gone by, or like empires past and present as they exploit their colonies.

The American empire uses film the way Spain's Catholic kings used religion.

It's the millions of dollars involved in film that drive Hollywood, not film itself ... It's not so much the big screen as it is the big bucks.

Hollywood is not a group of talented filmmakers whose art has earned a following, as with the German Expressionists, the New Wave, or the Italian School. Hollywood is an industry, and just like manufacturing, it is market-driven. The movie industry exploits film the way others exploit wood or aluminium.

Hollywood cares more about making money than making movies.

Hollywood is a multinational entertainment cartel that does business in every market around the world.

In building its worldwide oligopoly, Hollywood has stifled the rich creativity that one would expect from having so many creators around the world had the majors not lured them away and assimilated them or eliminated any chance for success in their own market.

For great talents, there was no salvation to be found outside of Hollywood.

The World As a Film Reel

For the big seven, the Earth is small and round like a film reel; it must be conquered: money flows with the black strips of celluloid, which intertwine and weave their way around the planet, always returning to the source of the Holy Wood.

All reels lead to Hollywood. And every effort is made to ensure that that's how things stay. Hollywood has progressively built a system capable of controlling film markets worldwide, with the ongoing support of the American government. Case in point, when the U.S. decided to support the reconstruction of Europe after the Second World War with the Marshall Plan, one of the conditions it imposed was that European theatres put no limits on American film (the Blum-Byrnes accord). It was a difficult condition to refuse at the time, and it demonstrated Washington and Hollywood's desire to conquer the world.

Today, film production around the world offers up the same scores from year to year:

> India: leading producer worldwide with 764 films
>   in 1999, 952 in 2001, 1,000 currently
> The United States: 500 to 650
> Japan: 270
> China (including Hong Kong): 230
> The Philippines: 220
> France: 181 in 1999, 200 since 2001

This is the environment in which the big seven and their hangers-on operate as a cartel, united in political and commercial lobbying in Washington and united when global distribution networks are at stake.

This is how American film captures 90% of box-office receipts even though it produces only 15% of the world's movies: the effectiveness of the system is hard to deny! Jack Valenti, the MPAA's president for 36 years, drove the point home himself: "The movie industry alone has a surplus balance of trade with every single country in the world. I don't believe another American enterprise can make that statement."[5]

You may remember an interview with Jane Fonda, a very committed, left-wing actress in the 1970s and a Vietnam War protestor, who was taken aback when a European journalist raised the question of American imperialism; she had never considered the possibility of stealth imperialism.

The well-known cultural exception brandished by a number of countries, France in particular, is constantly under attack by the Americans in international negotiations on trade and the free circulation of goods. In this sense, Hollywood is the ultimate symbol of ultraliberalism and globalization—the dream of North American businesspeople.

Hollywood sees the entire world as a domestic market, an integrated group of territories managed from its California headquarters relayed by satellite offices in strategic locations throughout the world. The MPAA, which was created in the aftermath of the Second World War and replaced by the Motion Picture Export Association (MPEA), chose a 35 mm reel in the centre of a globe as its symbol, like a pupil in the centre of an eye, revealing its hegemonic aspirations and how it wants to realize its planetary vision. From its head office in Los Angeles, the MPAA manages offices in Washington, Brussels, New Delhi, Rio de Janeiro, Singapore, Mexico, Toronto, and Jakarta. Plus, United International Pictures (Paramount Universal) maintains a presence through its own offices and through a variety of alliances and licences in over 200 countries, more countries than there are in the United

Nations! In English Canada, which has no movie border separating it from the U.S. and which adds another 10% to American distribution networks, independent Canadian films account for only 1.5% of box-office receipts in theatres.

Of course, Hollywood has a unique advantage in this regard. Not only does it have the largest domestic market in the world, which, alone, makes it a financial powerhouse, but it also has an enormous natural market of English speakers, ripe for the picking by distributors. These are generally countries with a high standard of living, where ticket sales for movies are brisk.

Unlike some theorists, I do not suggest that the Americans have dumped their movies at cut-rate prices on distribution networks around the world to impose their culture. On the contrary, they have carefully planned and applied commercial strategies to generate the most profit possible from so-called secondary markets.

Hollywood says that the American public doesn't want to see dubbed or subtitled foreign films and uses this as a pretext to either refuse to distribute foreign films or to require that they be remade, but it does not have the same scruples when it exports its English-language productions to foreign markets. International audiences simply have to learn to like original versions or get used to dubbing and subtitling. Estimates are that in 2000, 805 of the American films in circulation around the world were in English. However, the big seven are interested in the idea of producing in foreign languages to consolidate their market share, and Sony is leading the way, particularly in co-productions that receive foreign government subsidies, a condition of the film being made.

Many movies have already turned a profit on the North American market before they are distributed to foreign markets to generate additional profits. However, the size of the budgets for blockbusters—movies that cost more than

$100 million—are such that guaranteed access to foreign markets is sometimes necessary to ensure a return on investment and profits that can compensate for the risks and even the losses on films that flop.

Plus, there are so many American productions that they fill the demand of the domestic market without having to bring in foreign productions, something that does not happen in other countries, except for in India. The majors are criticized for their protectionism, but the reality is that they simply don't need to import movies to ensure that screens are fully programmed! And simply by blocking good foreign films, they banish them to marginal art or experimental networks, where their runs are guaranteed to be short.

Politics

Political correctness is something that has characterized Hollywood throughout its history (notwithstanding the considerable production of porno films, which falls outside the same official Puritanism).

In 1930, the Association of Motion Picture Producers and Distributors of America—the ancestor to the MPAA—and the censorship office adopted the Motion Picture Production Code, known as the Hays Code. The preamble reads, tellingly, "Motion picture producers recognize the high trust and confidence which have been placed in them by the people of the world and which have made motion pictures a universal form of entertainment."[6]

And the first articles affirm the principles of this God-fearing form of entertainment:

1. No picture shall be produced that will lower the moral standards of those who see it. Hence the sympathy of the audience should never be

thrown to the side of crime, wrongdoing, evil or sin.

2. Correct standards of life, subject only to the requirements of drama and entertainment, shall be presented.

3. Law, natural or human, shall not be ridiculed, nor shall sympathy be created for its violation.[7]

What follows is a series of headings for sensitive or forbidden topics: crime, coarse language, blasphemy, sex, belly buttons, suggestive dancing, ridiculing religion, poor taste in the portrayal of bedrooms ("the treatment of bedrooms must be governed by good taste and delicacy"[8]), disrespect for national pride ("the use of the flag shall be consistently respectful"[9]), poor taste in movie titles, and other distasteful subjects.

Happy endings became a moral constraint for all stories, whether emotional or historical dramas.

Later, Jack Valenti happily replaced the Hays Code with the Rating System, which simply classifies productions according to criteria related to the age of the audience.

Of course, one of the most striking moments in the history of film was the anti-communist witch hunt in the aftermath of the Second World War. It was the 1950s and McCarthyism was raging. A special committee of the U.S. Congress asked producers, directors, actors, and others the question: Are you now or have you ever been a member of the Communist Party?

"Our job, as Americans and as Republicans," Senator Joseph McCarthy said at his party's convention in 1952, "is to dislodge the traitors from every place where they've been sent to do their traitorous work."

Major actors came under suspicion and were blacklisted and banished from Hollywood simply for denouncing the harassment or refusing to answer the committee's question.

Since then, plenty of blockbusters have had the appearance of following marching orders from Washington or the Pentagon. The big seven regularly produce patriotic films in praise of America. Michael Bay's *Pearl Harbor* (2001) had a $150 million budget. There hasn't been a film made yet about the World Trade Center and September 11, but no doubt it will come, and it will have a slightly different feel than Michael Moore's *Fahrenheit 9/11*; the only reason it hasn't been made yet is probably due to legal issues with the victims' families.[10] It's hard to believe that it was mere coincidence that *America's Heart and Soul* and *The Alamo* were released in July 2004. The first, a documentary, just so happens to have been distributed by Buena Vista, part of the Walt Disney group, which refused to distribute *Fahrenheit 9/11*. It was released four weeks after Michael Moore's documentary, on July 4, Independence Day. The film is a portrayal of Middle America and the extraordinary stories of little people who are the heart and soul of the U.S.A. Walt Disney maintained that the close release dates were pure coincidence, but it did immediately organize a special screening a stone's throw from the Capitol for Move America Forward, a group started by Republicans in June 2004 in response to *Fahrenheit 9/11*. The group is "committed to supporting America's efforts to defeat terrorism and supporting the brave men and women of our Armed Forces"[11]—the invitation to the screening of the film went on to add, "unlike the negative and misleading story line of Michael Moore's *Fahrenheit 9/11*."[12] The film *The Alamo* celebrated American nationalism and the patriotism of the U.S. army, at the very moment the Pentagon and the CIA were taking a hit over the Iraq war and the army was having difficulty recruiting new soldiers for combat. The movie, which is set in Texas, tells the story of 200 Texans—men of all races united for the future of Texas—who in 1836 resisted the Mexican army for 13 days. The movie features all the

Hollywood clichés, including American heroes like Davy Crockett. "Only for Bush's fans!" an audience member commented on the web, and another said, "A great film!!! A must-see!!! Lots of true historical facts!!!"

Twentieth Century, owned by Fox, falls under the political control of Rupert Murdoch. Fox TV stations, in particular Fox News, have echoed George W. Bush's Republican party line to such an extent that the 2004 documentary *Outfoxed: Rupert Murdoch's War on Journalism* criticized this collusion. Hollywood is very much engaged in politics—American, of course, and, these days, preferably Republican.

But no matter what party is in power, the collusion between American capitalism and patriotism has been a constant. Jack Valenti himself is a former special advisor to Democratic president Lyndon Johnson. The United States is the only country in the world where filmmakers release patriotic movies every single year, particularly in time for its national holiday. If this sort of movie were released in France for July 14, it would be immediately torn apart by critics and would have no hope at the box office.

To promote their exports abroad, in 1918 producers were successful in obtaining the Webb-Pomerene Act, which exempts them from American antitrust laws in foreign markets, so long as they do not harm other members. In other words, producers are allowed to form a cartel to consolidate their exports. And that's exactly what the MPAA did, with Jack Valenti clearly identifying the objective: he wanted to ensure that American movies, TV shows, and video cassettes could circulate freely and unfettered around the world on markets that are open to competition. And to protect and develop its global hegemony, the MPAA has the unconditional support of the Department of Commerce. According to the European Audiovisual Observatory, in 2001, 66% of feature films distributed around the world were American, and of the 20 most-watched films in the world, 12 were American and 5 were co-produced with the United States.

The objection can be made that, among the majors, the Sony Group is Japanese, Fox is Australian (News Corp), and Universal Studios used to be Canadian when it was owned by the Bronfmans, then became French-owned, when it was bought by Vivendi, before changing hands again. And in this game of musical chairs, one could even imagine the big seven being turned over to foreign hands: it wouldn't change the machine, given how strong, integrated, effective, and profitable it is for owners. Neither Sony nor News Corp have challenged the system; on the contrary, they have imposed the same structure in Japan and Australia, for the very simple reason that movie-making is a licence to print money, which the majors don't want to let expire!

We are in the age of cultural capitalism, as many have already noted. Jeremy Rifkin has rightly pointed out that in the digital age capitalism depends less on natural resources, real estate, and tools of productivity than on the creation and exchange of cultural experiences. This is most definitely the case with movies, and the film industry was one of the first industries to move to cultural capitalism. Since then, the priority has been consumer demand. Market analyses are conducted to better profile products, successful products are reused, massive investment is made in advertising, and companies try to capture market share. Rifkin points to "an even larger transformation occurring in the nature of the capitalist system. We are making a long-term shift from industrial production to cultural production. More and more cutting-edge commerce in the future will involve the marketing of a vast array of cultural experiences ... "[13] We will be in a state of cultural hypercapitalism. Hollywood's global imperialism provides a vivid, loathsome example. For Rifkin, cultural capitalism is the supreme stage of capitalist civilization. It's a brilliant idea, but it puts tourism on the same level as film. And according to Rifkin, the Benjamin Franklin of the new capitalism, the difference between culture, communication, communion, and commerce is barely noticeable. That pretty much says it all. This is a principle that Hollywood has always understood and applied to film, well before Rifkin was born. And it should also be credited along with McDonald's and other cultural experiences that are symbols of the American way of life.

The U.S. imposes its hegemony around the world through military force more often than we would like. But more than the Romans, who used routes and centurions, the greatest power in the world today uses the economy, technoscience, and cultural exports to build its empire.

During GATT negotiations in 1995, Jack Valenti reportedly laughed out loud when a French bureaucrat pointed out that the United States already controlled 90% of the world film market and asked what more he wanted: 100%, of course! When, in 1987, Canadian Minister of Communications Flora MacDonald wanted to impose a Canadian content policy that would have had Canadian movies make up 15% of the films exhibited in Canada, she faced such tough lobbying from Jack Valenti that her bill was abandoned. Today, Canadian films represent less than 5% of movies shown on Canadian screens—a happy ending for Americans, who definitely know their own strength.

Commercial Infiltration Strategies

The big seven's commercial strategy has two facets: capturing markets and eliminating the competition. Their hegemony is based on massive investment, which offers the advantage of a decisive initial strike force. Their strategy lets them occupy the market and marginalize independent and national film from other countries, damaging them and their excellent productions: less money for creation, less promotion, and limited opportunity for revenue, which perpetuates and reinforces a vicious cycle. The situation has virtually wiped out film production in many countries, even in Italy, a country that has contributed so much to the history of film. The big seven therefore have a clear path and can buy local distribution networks at a good price to ensure that they have a virtual monopoly in the distribution of their own films. The free market serves them as they see fit and inflicts their movies on audiences in these countries.

The Numbers Tell the Story

In 1990, Hollywood earned 77.4% of box-office revenues in Europe: 58% in France, 91.5% in Ireland, and 93% in Great Britain. On the other hand, foreign films in the U.S. account for no more than 2% of revenues.

In 1991, Hollywood earned revenues of around $18 billion on the American market and $11.5 billion on international markets, $4 billion of them in Europe; in other words, almost 43% of total revenue came from abroad!

Canadian James Cameron's *Titanic* (1997), the film with the biggest production budget in the history of cinema, estimated at more than $200 million, turned out to be an excellent investment, because it generated worldwide revenue of $1.83 billion! Even in France, it attracted 20.6 million viewers, breaking Gérard Oury's 1996 French record for *La grande vadrouille*, which attracted 17.7 million moviegoers. But from the point of view of the industry, *Titanic* has one fatal flaw: *Titanic 2* and *3* are not as likely to be made as are *Spiderman* sequels.

The U.S. produced 473 films in 2003, 198 of which came from the majors. The year 2003 was a good one, according to MPAA president Jack Valenti, because American films generated profits of $9.5 billion. And yet, 2003 was slightly less profitable than 2002, so far the best year financially in the history of cinema. And Jack Valenti was worried about the average production cost of films, $63.8 million—or an increase of 8.6% over 2002—with the cost of A-movies rising to a record $102.8 million!

According to a PricewaterhouseCoopers study, in Europe in 2003, this same film industry generated revenues of 57 billion euros in box-office receipts and 151.6 billion euros in television distribution—in other words, three times as much through TV! The same study predicted that in 2006 these numbers would increase to 70 and 187 billion euros respectively. Pay-TV stations are obviously investing more to be able to offer their viewers blockbusters as soon as possible, a source of revenue that independent producers just can't tap into.

The American film industry and its derivatives (DVD, television, etc.) make up the second largest industry in the U.S. in terms of exports after aeronautics. By all appearances, the big seven are on top of their game, in complete opposition to the predicted decline! Hollywood shares the arrogance of the Pentagon and has become the most exported symbol of America, along with McDonald's and Coca-Cola. Now that the Berlin Wall has fallen and the Cold War has ended, the industry no longer even has the excuse that it is providing representations of the free world in the face of communist dictatorships. Hollywood is now appearing for what it has always been: arrogant imperialism and movie neocolonialism.

The Survival of the Fittest As Liberal Virtue

The majors call their hegemony *virtue* and legitimacy for an entertainment industry that is devoid of cultural diversity: let the market decide (in their favour, of course). The purpose of this market approach is to leave foreign markets wide open to American products, doing away with any regulatory and fiscal obstacles in the name of the natural equilibrium of the economy, which is supposed to promote prosperity for all (and above all, obviously, the prosperity of Americans, which is a cause only they hold dear).

In fact, how can the market decide and the public choose, as is its right, when the market is monopolized by productions from the Hollywood cartel, which takes movie screens prisoner and prevents other films from being screened? It's a curious interpretation of freedom of choice: killing off the competition to create a monopoly. And it's a policy that is based officially on the U.S. Global Audiovisual Strategy set up with Washington, which is intended to

- fight quotas that governments could impose to protect their national film production
- promote deregulation with regards to foreign, and therefore American, investment
- increase partnerships, in particular with private audiovisual companies, and American investment in foreign countries, to allow for takeovers.

The majors always use this strategy of penetration. And as France's Jack Ralite pointed out in February 1997 in a *Monde diplomatique* article, "The American approach is also being developed in international organizations: first at the OECD, as part of the negotiations for the Multilateral Agreement on Investment (MAI), which is intended to promote the circulation of foreign investment and to do away with subsidies to domestic producers. The objective of the United States is to obtain domestic and European treatment for their investments in Europe, and therefore to have access to community aid systems [MEDIA Plus] as well as national aid (fonds de soutien en France)."[14] And the majors often look for commercial allies, even political allies. In Canada, on the

45

outskirts of the American empire, 2004 saw the pro-American Conservative Party announce that once in power it would reduce quotas protecting Canadian productions in order to promote competition and American investment, creating what they said would be a stronger commercial dynamic that would benefit Canada.

During GATT negotiations in 1993, Jack Valenti tried to put an end to quotas and financial measures to support national movie production, advocating complete free trade, cultural industries included. But he failed in the face of resistance from the European Union, particularly from France, which obtained an exemption for audiovisual productions, including film and television. The World Trade Organization (WTO), however, is under constant pressure from the United States to take another look at this cultural exception, or to chip away at it bit by bit, in spite of the firm position of countries such as France, China, South Korea, and, increasingly, Canada.

The MPAA and the main American cultural industry associations banded together to represent their common interests to the Entertainment Industry Coalition for Free Trade (EIC), the stated objective of which is "to educate policymakers about the importance of free trade for the US economy, the positive economic impact of international trade on the entertainment community, and the role of international trade negotiations in ensuring strong intellectual property protections and improved market access for our products and services."[15] And this is how the EIC is progressively capturing foreign markets, including through successive bilateral agreements, each of which praises the globalist virtues of the countries that one after the other have caved in to American harassment and handed over their domestic markets. The June 2003 signature of the U.S.-Chile and the U.S.-Singapore accords in quick succession resonated like a cry of victory.

The EIC's American spokesperson recognized Chile's international trade delegates for their tireless work on the international agreement that would mutually benefit both countries, and then repeated the speech the next day in Singapore and the day after that in Australia, and for each new consenting victim.

In France, the country of the cultural exception, Walt Disney/Buena Vista nonetheless signed a distribution agreement with Gaumont in 1992, and Twentieth Century Fox signed a distribution agreement with the UGC, which in return will see a few of its films distributed in the U.S.

The Resistance

Hollywood's attitude has prompted reactions in defence of cultural exemptions and quotas to protect national production in countries such as France, Spain, India, Egypt, Canada, and South Korea—countries where movie-making still exists. And while these countries have been able to get some recognition from the WTO for the cultural exemption for audiovisual productions, this may only be a temporary defeat in the eyes of the MPAA. Because while a number of important filmmakers stood up to condemn this imperialism, according to Jack Valenti, the quotas are the beginning of a cancer!

Countries whose governments have chosen to resist the onslaught of American productions through legislation and subsidies are the only ones succeeding in maintaining national production. At the slightest sign of weakness, the result of a loophole in an international agreement, a pro-American party taking power, or alliances or buyouts of local companies, the Hollywood steamroller will move in. This is the strategy Hollywood could use to muscle in on one of the European Union countries, and from that base, use the country's national logo of film production to cast its shadow over the Old Continent, taking advantage of laws that promote the free circulation of people, ideas, and products. Hollywood's eagle eye is piercing and ever vigilant. It's counting on the fact that one day its prey will fall into its clutches. The big seven use truly predatory strategies when it comes to foreign markets.

Resistance is possible, although there is still little of it. In France, which has 185 million moviegoers annually, national film production occupies up to 35–40% of the market; in spite of all the measures taken to support French cinema, the country hands over more than 50% of its screens to American films.

Quebec is an interesting example: while English Canada sees virtually only Hollywood films, in Quebec, given its cultural and linguistic differences from the North American empire, independent made-in-Quebec films account for 20–25% of box-office receipts. This is due to audience demand, audiences that appreciate and support Quebec movies, but it is also due to persevering government policy, now bearing fruit, and to private initiatives like the opening of new independent theatres. The lesson is that it can be done, even in the empire's backyard!

When South Korea established quotas requiring theatres to show South Korean films 146 days a year—less than one out of every two days—Jack Valenti opposed the move vigorously: "I am fighting that quota because I am an advocate of competition," he said. "We have the right to enter their market as much as they can enter the U.S. market. They just need to find a theater and distributor for it here. If a theater in Korea wants to show an American film, it should have the right to. Some theaters have to close because there are not enough Korean movies to keep them alive."[16] Valenti's words pretty much sum up the commercial cynicism of the Hollywood system.

Among the champions of resistance is France's national film body, the Centre national de la cinématographie—the CNC—which imposed a tax on box-office receipts the proceeds of which are redistributed to French producers in the form of advances for production. As a result, American box-office hits in France contribute to French productions in spite of themselves!

Given the way they operate, Americans are clearly a source of irritation around the world. The horrendous attack on the World Trade Center in New York, orchestrated by al-Qaida terrorists much like a Hollywood production, is a terrible irony, but it will go down in history as a sadly memorable symbol of the divide between the insolence of the rich in developed countries and the exasperation of humiliated peoples who want legitimacy and recognition of their diversity, but whose oil the American empire wants to control. Where Americans see the simple regulation of markets involving general deregulation under the guise of global free trade (which they themselves are constantly resisting with protectionist measures), anti-globalization grumbling is getting louder and spreading planet-wide.

Hollywood is therefore arousing increasing resistance by those who oppose American imperialism. All the "anti's" of the ultraliberal market economy and the defenders of cultural diversity oppose the big seven's system of market protectionism. George W. Bush's United States has created a virtually global anti-Americanism. Hollywood should pay attention to this growing current of hostility in defence of the right of difference.

Because the fact is that more than any other American industry, Hollywood has succeeded in achieving its global vision. And through an impending swing of the pendulum, the process of globalization will inevitably also become the trial of the big seven.

NOTES

5. Senate Committee on Governmental Affairs, *Privacy & Piracy: The Paradox of Illegal File Sharing on Peer-to-Peer Networks and the Impact of Technology on the Entertainment Industry: Statement of Jack Valenti*, September 30, 2003, http://www.senate.gov/~govt-aff/index.cfm?Fuseaction=Hearings.Testimony& HearingID=120&WitnessID=415

6. Arts Reformation.com, "The Motion Picture Production Code of 1930 (Hays Code)," http://www.artsreformation.com/a001/hays-code.html

7. Ibid.

8. Ibid.

9. Ibid.

10. Since the writing of this book, Paul Greengrass's *United 93* and Oliver Stone's *World Trade Center* were both released in 2006.

11. Move America Forward.org, "About Move America Forward," http://www.moveamericaforward.org/index.php/MAF/AboutUs

12. John M. Hubbell, "New Disney Film Takes Another View of U.S.: *America's Heart and Soul* a Contrast to *Fahrenheit 9/11*," *San Francisco Chronicle*, June 30, 2004.

13. Jeremy Rifkin, *The Age of Access: The New Culture of Hypercapitalism Where All of Life Is a Paid-for Experience* (New York: Jeremy P. Tarcher/Putnam, 2000), 7.

14. Jack Ralite, "Hollywood à l'offensive: cultures à vendre," *Le Monde diplomatique*, February 1997, 32.

15. David Johnson, Executive Vice President and General Counsel Warner Music Group, "U.S.-Chile and U.S.-Singapore Free Trade Agreements: Benefits to America's Entertainment Industries," testimony on behalf of the Entertainment Industry Coalition for Free Trade (EIC) before the Senate Finance Committee, June 17, 2003, 2.

16. MIT Communications Forum, "Movies in the Digital Age," April 8, 2004, http://web.mit.edu/comm-forum/forums/valenti.html

THE COGS OF HOLLYWOOD IMPERIALISM

Cogs: the word evokes antiquated technologies and describes the way Hollywood imperialism operates.

Universalism

Hollywood targets a transnational audience and to do so it must put out sufficiently *international* movie products (in the same sense that international cuisine refers to a cuisine with no marked flavours) shot on a wide variety of locations and palatable everywhere. Just as French culture did in its glory days of the 18th and 19th centuries, and as any dominant culture would, contemporary American culture tries to impose its vision and values on the whole world, values it believes to be superior to all others; American culture considers itself progress and a universal reference point. And it works! California has been called the social laboratory of the future, harbinger of what awaits other countries twenty years down the road. Edgar Morin's fascination with the culture led him into this trap in his *Journal de Californie*. Old Europe, the condescending characterization of George W. Bush's ministers of war, should bow before the superiority of the American model, revised and improved Texas-style.

In fact, Hollywood productions are presented as good stories well told, *normal* films, without any strong cultural references, except for easily recognizable stereotypes. All dominant ideologies appear to be obvious, natural, universal, in other words, invisible. There is no better example of this than Walt Disney movies for kids of all ages, which are seemingly as apolitical and acultural as the animal kingdom, but which many analyses have shown are laden with ideology and symbolism that echo conservative values.

The discourse of Hollywood productions is also simplistic: good battles evil and always prevails. Of course, good is invariably American, with courageous heroes—humanity's saviours—incarnating the nation's lofty values. These values are always explicit and highly praised at some point in the movie. For instance, in *Spiderman 2*, the hero loses his powers when he loses his faith, as a psychologist explains to him. And of course crime immediately increases by 75% in New York. His family consists of a mysterious old man and an elderly aunt who, at one point in the film, gives him a good talking-to, after which he regains his self-confidence and his life-saving power. Spiderman returns to saving children from burning buildings, pedestrians from oncoming cars, and passengers from runaway trains, and crime plummets once again! And of course, the film includes a love story to warm the cockles of the heart.

Hollywood producers create narratives that are easy to follow, even for audiences with limited education or recent immigrants who haven't yet mastered English. The way a film is made and the story's sensationalism and understandability are all factors in producing effective products for pop culture.

Laurent Gervereau, an authority on film and author of *Histoire du visuel au xxe siècle* (2003), shows how throughout most of the world, Hollywood, and not painting, has been setting the standard for female beauty since 1945. Stars like Marilyn Monroe, Audrey Hepburn, and their European doppelgangers Brigitte Bardot and Gina Lollobrigida defined what a young woman should be like: sensual but maternal, erotic but child-like, voluptuous but slim. As was the case with male standards of beauty, with James Dean, John Wayne, and particularly Marlon Brando. According to Gervereau, in the face of the socialist realism of the Communist Bloc and its worker heroes, these canons of beauty were used as propaganda to sell happiness and the American way of life.

Settings for films generally lack local colour, except for exotic films, in which the setting is like a postcard that can easily be appropriated in any theatre around the world.

Producers also ensure that their films are appropriate for all ages so that they can reach a family audience. They target children, knowing full well that their parents will accompany them to the movies. *Harry Potter* is a typical example of this. Movies regularly feature male and female heroes who span three generations—children, adults, and seniors—with plots that give each character a moment to shine.

The diversity of the human and physical landscape of the U.S., and the importance of the melting pot, from the outset meant that producers believed that to be a domestic success they had to find the common denominator and create family-oriented, simplistic movies, for heterogeneous audiences.

As a result, family movies are typically American and tend toward the universal, as French critic and filmmaker Éric Rohmer has noted longingly.[17] And this is precisely the strength of imperialism: it passes for universalism, all the better for conquering minds ... and foreign markets.

All that's left is to hold up American values as enviable and universal—as many do, including U.S. presidents and many foreign admirers—to legitimize the globalization of cinema. There are many who would give up diversity in culture and values to enjoy the pleasures of the rich and powerful.

The U.S. produces scarcely more than 600 films out of the 3,000 to 4,000 films produced worldwide every year, but the big seven has imposed its particular brand of film, with one-dimensional human emotions and adventures that combine spectacle and suspense. The success of the genre, however, must be placed within the context of the marketing efforts that determine the cocktail of ingredients that will have broad appeal.

The American-style movie has a very effective sales pitch built in: the much-flaunted, decades-long success of the American way of life that these movies show the world, incorporating symbols of wealth, power, energy and vitality, the pursuit of happiness, and the happy ending, seducing those who are deprived of these things—in other words, almost everyone. And justice, something else that so many people search for in vain, always prevails in the simplistic battles between good and evil. The culture has a perpetually sunny discourse that appeals to doubters and sufferers. In other countries, most of the great films throughout the ages have had more complex discourses, marked by doubt, suffering, and misfortune, with its embittered victims. It's not surprising that the films of Woody Allen—the anti-Hollywood filmmaker if ever there was one—depicting an awkward man who is a magnet for failure and tortured by myriad questions, found their place only in New York, nor is it surprising that he wound up taking refuge in Europe.

The big seven sell the American dream—the dream of personal success—around the world. Wim Wenders says, "Would we find the American dream worldwide without movies? No other country in the world has sold itself so much through film, and spread its images, or its image of itself, so powerfully around the world."[18] The success of these films has created and consolidated attitudes and expectations of audiences, who have become accustomed to the formulas, asking for them over and over again like Valium, in spite of how repetitive they are.

America's fundamental myths, the Americanness that its movies convey, are very effective. And they have been abundantly described. Paul Warren summarizes them as follows: "Populism (anything that originates with the people is good), equality of opportunity, individualism tempered by mutual aid and neighbourly acts, the settlement of the West, the dichotomy of savagery/civilization and divine election ... "[19]

This explains why not only the middle class, but also the poor in developing countries and the masses who have long been deprived of any hope for freedom or quality of life, such as in post–Cultural Revolution China, are big fans of American film! China will have to wait for the next generation for resistance and a renewed quest for its own cultural values.

The majors have also systematically recruited filmmakers whose films they distributed have turned out to be hits. This practice has obviously increased their chances of leadership worldwide, but it has also contributed to the internationalization of their productions. The U.S. is a country of immigrants of all origins, and the culture itself is a strange hybrid of multiculturalism dominated by the unifying dream of power. American movies are therefore more likely than those of other countries to appeal to different, or so-called universal, sensibilities, and to resonate worldwide.

Hollywood sells the Americanization/globalization of culture around the world, just like it sells gum and cigarettes. But is this really the most basic type of story, the most straightforward, natural style there is?

Of course not, but it's a default style. It's the style of the largest, and therefore the lowest, common denominator, for the most international audience possible. It is like a restaurant menu in an international airport, meant to attract everyone without displeasing anyone, an American-African-Chinese-

Indian-Russian-Canadian restaurant, the characteristic vacuousness of which manages to be as uncharacteristic as possible. Hollywood and Coca-Cola have the same taste!

It is the taste of those who recommend thinking globally and acting locally, as the well-known environmental slogan goes.

The Pentagon, Coca-Cola, and Hollywood have joined forces to impose the American way of life and thinking, which they mistakenly identify with global symbols of freedom, democracy, and progress, to dominate markets and minds. Oil magnate Marvin Davis bought Fox in 1981, and Coca-Cola bought Columbia Pictures in 1982, proving that American film opens the door to other products, such as jeans.

Is this the triumph of humanism? A convincing universalism? It's curious then that Hollywood stars are almost exclusively white ...

Bread, Circus, and Movies

Hollywood *is* movies, but in the sense that it is an entertainment industry that controls the quality of its product and the regularity with which it is delivered to the market. To accomplish this, it needs seasoned, interchangeable filmmakers. There are exceptions to the rule of course, filmmakers who have managed to make their mark, such as Alfred Hitchcock. But the fact that Warner Bros could change directors for each of the *Harry Potter* movies is telling.

All industries need to market standardized products that offer consistent quality and appeal, whether we're talking about shoes or cars. That is precisely what the big seven does with movies, telling the same stories, with the same stars, the same technical quality, and the same emotions. Like the wrong grade of potatoes, atypical movies don't make the cut.

When in spite of this homogenizing system, there are non-standardized must-sees that make money, the big seven snap them up to control their distribution through their own network of theatres. And it's this small show of tolerance that quells the risk of animosity toward the system.

One of the big seven's production strategies is to divide work among subcontractors with expertise in screenwriting, sets, casting, shooting, special effects, editing, or sound, in what has been referred to as a division of labour, assembly-line production, or rather, post-Taylorism, to highlight the flexibility of managing production this way, as the big seven draw resources from the cluster of satellite companies that orbit them. This division of labour ensures consistency in the style of production.

This cultural product cum mass entertainment excludes anything that doesn't sell, doesn't have mass appeal, or is too original, preferring visual effects and popular emotions. Hollywood film is a mass medium that is devoid of political or social content. Experimentation and creativity are sacrificed to satisfy the greatest number. Movies need to sell to the widest audience possible and entertainment obviously sells better than asking hard questions: spectacle attracts larger crowds than art and experimental film. Bread and games, said the Roman emperors, to satisfy the masses. It's not surprising that Hollywood films are so similar to games at a Roman circus, be it *Ben Hur*, *The Last Samurai* with Tom Cruise, or others that feature modern-day gladiators like Superman, Spiderman, and Batman. "We need Rambo," the president and ex-actor Ronald Reagan once said in talking about a foreign conflict. But Rambo, Terminator, and Robocop are nothing more than modern-day versions of Roman gladiators.

For close to a century, Hollywood has been building an empire on which the sun never sets, using a very effective

strategy developed by the majors. Now let's look at the parts
of the machine, the kinks of which they worked out on the
domestic market before implementing it worldwide.

Blockbusters

The big seven have adopted a widespread production strategy
of spectacular big-budget mega-productions, for which they
alone have the means. They have also adopted equally
staggering promotional campaigns that are extremely
effective at attracting audiences and symbolically continuing
the tradition of Hollywood superiority. The production and
promotional costs for these films necessitate, to limit the
financial risk, conforming to the safest, cookie-cutter models
that in-depth studies of audience expectations suggest. The
end result is primarily popular movies that trot out the same
type of story, the same mise-en-scène and narrative, in as
many versions as possible, all of which are inevitably boring
for more demanding moviegoers.

This strategy turned out films like *Jaws* in the 1970s, and
more recently, *Titanic*, movies that deal with the fears that
most preoccupy us at the end of the millennium; then there
are science fiction movies and A-movies such as *Independence
Day*, *Mars Attacks!*, *The Matrix*, *The Last Samurai*, *The Lord of
the Rings*, *The Day After Tomorrow*, and *Spiderman*. Cheaper
films, or B-movies, ride on the coattails of these blockbusters
to fill theatres and provide considerable returns, in proportion
with their more modest budgets of course.

Jack Valenti used to tell anyone who would listen that if
other producers were less successful than those of the MPAA,
it was simply because they refused to take the same financial
risks. In fact, in 2000, the average cost of an American feature
film was estimated at $55 million, whereas the average
European production cost only $10 million.

What Valenti never pointed out, however, is Hollywood's slick marketing machine. A film is first released in major theatres, where it earns its initial receipts and where, more importantly, it establishes its value on the market according to how well it is received by critics and the media. Then twenty weeks later, it is sold on DVD for home viewing. The third step is to sell it again twenty weeks later to pay-per-view stations, which generates considerable revenue, then to cable TV, which also pays high royalties, and finally to commercial TV and the general public. This process is then repeated in foreign markets as many times over as possible. A film can triple or quadruple its box-office receipts, on top of revenues from tie-in merchandise. Total revenues for a hit can be as high as $400 million domestically and up to $1.8 billion on the international market, compensating for possible flops among other major productions. Apparently, this is an unbeatable business model. A film's release in theatres is therefore just the trigger for the marketing of a chameleon-like product, which, due to the enormous promotional budget for its release, can meet with limited success in theatres, but can catch up when it goes to DVD earlier and through the sale of tie-in merchandise.

The worst thing about blockbusters is that if they do well financially, they are followed by any number of sequels until the story is worn threadbare. Just like in the automobile industry, if a model sells well, it is re-released virtually unchanged, or only cosmetically changed, for years to come.

Spiderman, released in 2002, is a warmed-over version of *Superman*, which was a huge hit. Instead of being a young journalist, the hero is a student and photojournalist who also protects the residents of New York from evil. Both characters dress in magical costumes, but rather than flying with a cape, Spiderman scales the façades of skyscrapers and gets around by shooting long strands of spider silk, bringing to mind another evil-battling hero: Tarzan, who swung from vine to vine. And as a finale, Hollywood has remade *King Kong*, with the beauty in the clutches of the beast at the top of the Empire State Building.

Spiderman generated box-office revenues of \$114.9 million and total revenue of \$404 million in North America, \$806 million worldwide, placing it second worldwide among highest-grossing hits. Based on these results, Sony Columbia Pictures chose to reoffend with *Spiderman 2* in July 2004, which was released simultaneously to 4,152 theatres in North America. *Spiderman 2* apparently cost \$200 million to make. The stakes are high, but so are the expected profits. The eve of the fourth of July long weekend was chosen as the release date. And, the day after *Spiderman 2* was released in theatres, Activision US launched the video game based on the film, issuing two million copies for the American market alone. The game lets players pretend to be Spiderman, attacking the evil Dr. Octopus and saving innocent children from peril.

One of Hollywood's formulas is to exploit all of the derived rights from a movie's intellectual property, whether in the form of theme parks, merchandise, action figures in cereal boxes and on T-shirts, and games and ads of all sorts.

One very effective business strategy is to buy the universal rights to a book that has sold well internationally. Marvel Enterprises owns the rights to the Spiderman character, which was created in 1962, one of approximately 5,000 different characters that the company has acquired a virtual monopoly over. Fifteen million copies of the *Spiderman* comic book are sold each year in 75 countries, translated into 22 languages. The comic strip is reprinted in 500 newspapers worldwide. The adaptation for television, produced by Sony Pictures, is broadcast on 124 channels, representing 86% of the American market.

Likewise, the bookstore success of J. K. Rowling's *Harry Potter*, which over the course of five successive titles sold more than 250 million copies (*The Prisoner of Azkaban* sold 1.8 million copies in Great Britain its first day on sale), paved the way for the worldwide success of the *Harry Potter* films produced by Warner Bros Studios. And we're only at the third film, while J. K. Rowling is writing the sixth instalment, and a seventh has been announced! These rights also apply for impressive sales on DVD, sales for pay-per-view and regular TV, and the marketing of innumerable tie-in products; it's a veritable magical gold mine, with no genie or dragon defending it from the greedy hands of the industry.

Movies As Events

Distributors systematically invest heavily to promote their movies. According to the MPAA, in 2003, the average cost of production for a movie was $63.8 million (an increase of 8.6% over 2002), and the average cost of the release was $39 million (an increase of 28% over 2002), for an average total of more than $100 million per movie! In 2003, the big seven apparently spent $6.76 billion in advertising. The majors start their advertising campaigns six months, and sometimes one year, in advance. This lead time gives them a strike force that independent producers can only dream of, making dominating the international market an effortless task. As a result, there is little room left for promoting independent films. Sometimes producers ruin the financial prospects of a movie by trying to compete with Hollywood movies on promotion. But they don't make the same mistake twice. More limited promotion budgets mean that independent films often don't benefit from the secondary markets of DVD and tie-in merchandise. And because they don't have a powerful enough promotional campaign, they have to settle for less when sold to television. As a result, these pictures only exist through government subsidies, which the MPAA criticizes as an affront to "free" competition!

These massive promotional campaigns force theatre owners to settle for the release dates the majors set and submit to the requirements of distribution contracts: it's take it or leave it, and theatre owners have no choice but to take it in this highly competitive market.

A-movies are film events when they open in theatres, with a media celebration to ensure their box-office success and strong performance in the later stages of their career. The logic of the majors is consistent and extremely effective: it's the power of money over the power of film.

Block Booking and Blind Booking

The purpose of block booking, which has been used on the American market since the 1920s, is to control distribution networks. And the practice is stronger than ever today. Thanks to their de facto monopoly, the big seven can impose all of their films on theatre owners. The owners have no choice, because if they want A-movies the day they are released, they have to rent B-movies at the same time, which they have to pay for of course, and which they will therefore screen. This system is called blind booking, meaning that theatre owners have to make a blind choice of movies that are imposed on them. And it's why good theatres sometimes show bad movies, to the surprise of moviegoers. It's not the theatre owner's fault; it's the system's fault. Even the worst movies the majors produce are guaranteed minimal receipts through this underhanded system. Flops just don't flop financially.

The movies that are shown in theatres therefore depend entirely on the decisions of Hollywood moguls. Basically, it doesn't matter that antitrust laws prohibit producers from buying up all the theatres in the United States. They can buy them in other countries. And they don't even need to control them through ownership to control what is shown on their screens and to ensure that they have as many screens as they want in virtually every theatre. The abominable practice of block booking results in the complete and consenting enslavement of theatre owners.

Of course, block booking is much more flexible in Canada than in many other countries. But Quebec's association of theatre owners, the Association québécoise des propriétaires de salles, will not soon forget the conditions that Fox wanted to impose on it to show George Lucas's final *Star Wars* film: 70% of box-office receipts and a minimum of four weeks' screen time, in the best theatre! Fox was confident, but the purchasing cooperative refused, and the film did not open in theatres that were members of the association. But how many in other countries could stand up to Fox over a money-maker like *Star Wars*, which the public no doubt will clamour to see?

The Star System

For their first pictures—such as the first feature film, Edwin S. Porter's 1903 *Great Train Robbery*—production houses used anonymous actors, out of fear, it seems, of creating reputations and therefore having to enter into more expensive contracts. By 1909, Hollywood had understood that the star system would contribute to the success of its films. The star system also led to the publication of *Motion Picture Story Magazine* and *Photoplay*, magazines that deified stars, a sort of royal family for working-class Americans, giving them a leading role to play in society. The popular figures, with their faces frozen in seductive or sad smiles depending on the instructions of their masters, lived in luxurious homes that could be spied through iron gates at the end of shady yards scattered throughout the famous neighbourhood of Beverly Hills. The public fretted over their love lives, their whims, and their weaknesses, all of which were discussed at length in well-controlled gossip rags. The stars were offered to the sacrificial admiration of the masses through rituals and red carpets. They were the Hollywood symbol of success and the American dream, a dream that everyone wants to identify with.

Edgar Morin remarks in his book *Les stars* (1957), "Stars are the product of a dialectic of the personality: actors impose their personalities on the heroes they play and heroes impose their personalities on the actors. This superimposition creates a hybrid being: the star."[20]

Morin reminds us that when we talk about the myth of the star, we are talking first and foremost about the deification process actors go through on the way to becoming idols. They are the gods and heroes of the Holy Wood, with their stereotypical airs: Rudolph Valentino, the irresistible Gary Cooper, the enigmatic James Dean, the big-hearted cowboy John Wayne, the disillusioned Humphrey Bogart, Buster Keaton, Cary Grant, Mickey Rooney, Clark Gable, Paul Newman, Rock Hudson, Robert Mitchum, Frank Sinatra, Burt Lancaster, Marlon Brando, and Kirk Douglas. And there are the goddesses of Mount Olympus: Jeanette MacDonald, Gloria Swanson, Marlene Dietrich, Claudette Colbert, Marilyn Monroe, Ava Gardner, Jayne Mansfield, Liz Taylor, Greta Garbo, and Judy Garland. The star system let the rapturous masses glimpse turquoise-watered pools, milk-filled baths with gold faucets, and convertible limousines where gods and goddesses travelled as in a dream, symbols of wealth and beauty. This is how the Hollywood myth was created to shine its artificial chrome all over the planet. Morin shows how stars became the raw material of an industry. They were the product the big seven sold to the entire world, because famous actors made movies famous ... and profitable. The system sometimes went awry, as with the tragic deaths of Marilyn Monroe, Judy Garland, and James Dean, but these deaths only added to the myth. However, Morin goes on to state, "After 1960 the star system, which had transformed lead into gold and poison into honey, started to derail."[21] The system has paled since then, although some contemporary actors still shine within it, such as Julia Roberts, Meryl Streep, Glenn Close, Jack Nicholson, Robert De Niro, Al Pacino, Michael Douglas, Robert Redford, and Tom Cruise, who are excellent salespeople for Hollywood productions. And of course there is Lara Croft, a computer-generated superstar of the digital age, whose polygons manage to keep a promotional agency busy full time generating gossip that gets fans going as if she were a curvaceous flesh-and-blood star. There is such a need for deified fantasies that fans are satisfied with a simulation!

Question: Why do Canadian movies fill only 2% or 3% of theatres in English Canada?

- Because unlike in Quebec, there is no star system in English Canada.
- Why? Are there no beautiful women or handsome young men in English Canada?
- Of course there are! But they head south, because Hollywood offers movie stars $10–20 million for a film.
- It's only natural that Canadian films don't sell well. And it's only natural that good Canadian directors head south. So there are fewer Canadian films produced. It's only logical.

Paul Warren has performed a remarkable analysis of how the natural pseudo-simplicity of Hollywood narratives, sets, and above all close-ups of actors (or reaction shots), make it possible to participate live and in real time in the emotions of the stars, encouraging the identification of audience members with the heroes and heroines of the story.[22] He even points out that the reaction shot is part of the heritage of European fascist film, which Federico Fellini denounced in all his work.

Warren also shows very cleverly how the fluid and seemingly natural narrative that Hollywood movies use communicates American values, made to seem matter-of-fact to viewers, making the message even more effective because it is imperceptible: The more invisible the technique, the greater the power of movies ... the most basic form of screenwriting constitutes the highest form of ideological manipulation.[23]

The Oscars

Regardless of what Andy Warhol said, a few seconds of fame can't hurt the system, particularly when the event is broadcast worldwide. The Oscars are much envied by the movie industries around the world. Awarded every year since 1927 by the Academy of Motion Picture Arts and Sciences, the Oscars create major internal battles because they have so much influence over box-office receipts and DVD and television sales. Thus, even within conglomerates, there have been recent rivalries. The Independent Feature Project protested the viewing practices of the American Awards Association juries, which had a tendency to reserve the Oscars for its own members by limiting the viewing of independent productions, following an MPAA requirement that used the pretext of fighting DVD pirating (the screener ban case). The case was finally settled out of court; Jack Valenti didn't want to make waves: "Let us be clear that our aim from the beginning was to ensure the viability and survival of this industry—for independents and non-independents alike."[24] And those in charge of the coalition of plaintiffs reiterated their desire to have "the MPAA engage in an ongoing process in which all constituencies of the industry are guaranteed a voice in the development of effective, fair and legal antipiracy policies."[25]

35 mm Reels

Ah! The sacred reel! It is without a doubt the lead actor in the Hollywood story. Thirty-five mm reels are among the keys to the big seven's control over distribution networks. While film post-production is now entirely digital, the majors insist now more than ever that the final master print be transferred to 35 mm rather than remain in digital format. Why, when producing this master can cost on average around $60,000 for a feature, and prints can cost $2,500 or $3,000, even up to $6,000 if the movie is dubbed or subtitled?

Distributors are the ones who have to absorb the cost of these prints, to make them available simultaneously in theatres the day a movie is released, even though the distributor has no guarantee that the movie will be a success, and many of these reels end up in landfills soon after the film comes out.

Film reels weigh up to 40 kg each and are extremely expensive to ship and insure, often costing up to $500 each, and they are awkward to handle. For a long time, they were even dangerous, because the film could ignite (just think of Cinéma Paradiso).

Celluloid and film are also fragile and vulnerable to mechanical friction. They get scratched and wear out quickly, and the quality of projection, on which the MPAA bases its sacrosanct argument, soon deteriorates.

These high costs obviously mean having to limit 35 mm film distribution to major theatre networks, where box-office receipts compensate for the fixed costs of the prints.

Distributors cannot turn a profit in theatres with fewer than 200 people, and without new films, smaller theatres can't build a loyal clientele. As a result, small independent theatres have been progressively disappearing for years.

The negative impact of distribution via 35 mm reels is considerable and has been deadly for large portions of film production. Filmmakers have wanted to move away from 35 mm before. They hoped to win their freedom through 16 mm and then through video. But these formats couldn't stand up to Hollywood competition because of their substandard definition on the big screen.

Hollywood's control of the industry through the 35 mm reel has directly contributed to the demise of thousands of small theatres and has helped marginalize art and experimental film, national cinema, auteur film, and activist film, including short features and documentaries.

Ironically, the 35 mm reel remains the symbol of the glory of film as an industry, but has become the instrument of its death as an art. As Björn Koll said recently, "In Germany, if 10 copies of a movie are released, they are first distributed to major centres. It takes six months for a movie to arrive at the village next door. There is nothing democratic about this. It is anything but egalitarian. Plus, this form of distribution is expensive. In the end, theatres close. And when, through some miracle, a movie manages to arrive in one of these theatres, the print is in such a state that it can no longer be viewed."[26]

The cost of these reels also limits the ability of independent distributors to release a film in larger theatre networks, because they do not have the means to provide the number of copies necessary. And if a film is a hit, the extra prints needed can't be produced in time, preventing a film for which there is demand from reaching a wider audience.

Why, in spite of all the major inconveniences, is Hollywood still making a religion out of 35 mm reels? Officially, it's in the name of image quality. And when digital technology matches, and surpasses, the definition of film, the spectre of piracy is raised, which the cost of prints protects against. But what goes unsaid is much more strategic, and this religion goes back much earlier than the recent problem of pirating. The fact is that distribution via 35 mm reels has always made it possible to control distribution and therefore theatre screens. This is a curious destiny for a 35 mm perforated celluloid strip covered with silver-based emulsion. The problem is not a new one! Since the era of George Eastman, Kodak film has been a major issue for producers. Even Georges Méliès had to deal with it when, for example, he bought film in England and discovered when he received it that it was not pre-perforated. As a result he had to invent a machine so that he could shoot. Fortunately he was the son of a leather craftsman, which went a long way toward solving the problem.

Thirty-five mm reels allow Hollywood to control theatres, open and close box offices remotely, and eliminate any flexibility in the timing of screenings and any liberties taken with its films.

Zoning

Following a decision of the DVD Forum, the big seven today use the same zoning technique for the DVD market that they dreamed up in 1910 for the distribution of their films on the American market: controlling the calendar of release dates according to the geographical zones of the market. This protects them from resellers importing DVDs that have been launched in other countries, but not at home. To do this, the majors have broken down markets into geographical territories, ensuring that DVDs are not compatible with different types of DVD players sold from one market to the next. The fact that they are powerful enough to force equipment manufacturers to meet such requirements is telling. But what else can they do, when blockbusters that are released in the United States can be sold freely for a dollar per DVD in Asia two days later, even before the film hits the theatres, which is what happened with *Harry Potter* in 2001.

———

NOTES

17. Éric Rohmer, "Rediscovering America," in *The 1950s: Neo-Realism, Hollywood, New Wave*, vol. 1 of *Cahiers du Cinéma*, ed. Jim Hiller (Cambridge, Mass.: Harvard University Press, 1985), 88–93.

18. Émile Baron, "L'empire et les barbares (1)," Cadrage.net, 2001. http://www.cadrage.net/films/alombredhollywood/alombredhollywood.html

19. Paul Warren, *Le secret du star-system américain: le dressage de l'oeil* (Montreal: L'Hexagone, 2002), 12–13.

20. Edgar Morin, *Les Stars* (Paris: Seuil, 1972), 170.

21. Ibid., 158.

22. Warren, *Le secret du star-system américain*.

23. Ibid., 67.

24. David Rooney and Cathy Dunkley, "MPAA, Indie Org OK Screener Compromise," Variety.com, March 29, 2004, http://www.variety.com/article/VR1117902525?categoryid=1683&cs=1

25. Ibid.

26. Luc Perreault, "Un example européen: Docuzone," *La Presse*, May 23, 2004.

HollywooD: The Future of Cinema Is Digital

Illuminated, animated images projected on a screen before an audience: this is what defines film at its most basic level. Take away any one of these elements and we are no longer talking about film. And yet, film is not necessarily bound to the invention that is at its source—silver-based emulsion film on a strip of perforated celluloid, unwound in a projector. Other systems are possible, as long as they can achieve the same result. But what is intrinsic to film is that it has always played with numbers, whether the optical combinations of the camera and projector, or 24 frames per second. While photography and cinema both have their fair share of film lovers, film as a physical object does not define either art form, both of which are moving to digital. Digital technology is not contrary to the nature of cinema, because cinema has always evolved with technology, just like books, painting, sculpture, architecture, and music have done; none of them has stopped being what they are as a result.

In *Cinema and Digital Media* (1996), Lev Manovich points out that the computer was initially a military technology, developed by Alan Turing to decrypt coded messages from the Germans, and it has since become a machine for multimedia images. But the device Turing invented to read and combine the information from perforated cards was a sort of notched-strip reader that was clearly inspired by film projectors.

Because of this, Manovich contends that the computer was born of film. And he even goes back to J. M. Jacquard's knitting machines at the beginning of the 19th century, which made it possible to produce patterns, even a portrait of Jacquard himself, whose sweaters became famous. Manovich rightly recalls the oft-forgotten existence of the other inventor of the computer, Berliner Konrad Zuse, who used 35 mm film reels to process his series of binary codes. The first Commodore computers used magnetic tape cassettes, like those used to record audio and video. The phone too, which is now also digital, started out on magnetic technology. There is, as a result, a certain continuity among these technologies.

Film and digital technology therefore have common origins. And both can simulate reality by manipulating space and time mechanically, chemically, optically, analogically, or digitally. As early as the 1890s, Georges Méliès's special effects were based on the ingenious manipulation of numbers, space, time, and rhythm. And if we accept 24 frames per second as an algorithm, we could even say that film has always been digital.

As early as 1982, Francis Ford Coppola's *One from the Heart*, a drama with plenty of special effects, heralded the arrival of electronic technology in film and a communications revolution. The story continued with the development of software for electronic music and visual effects—addressed at the beginning of this book—compression software, the internet, high-definition (HD) digital cameras, the first entirely digital shoots, and now digital distribution. We are still on the same continuum, closing the circle for end-to-end digital film.

Even before they could use high-definition digital cameras, filmmakers were increasingly opting for digital video, or DV, cameras. Danish filmmaker Lars von Trier chose DV to shoot *The Idiots* in 1998 and *Dancer in the Dark* in 1999, and Thomas Vinterberg used high definition in 1998 for *Festen*. When von Trier was awarded the Golden Palm at the Cannes Film Festival in 1999 with a film shot on digital video, a lot of filmmakers were won over. Wim Wenders publicly praised digital technology when he shot *The Ground Beneath Her Feet,* and Claude Miller did the same with *Of Woman and Magic* in 2000. He said that it was a new experience for him, and he believed it changed his entire approach to making the film.

More filmmakers are now choosing to shoot with digital video cameras: Agnès Varda (*The Gleaners and I,* 2000); Barbet Schroeder (*Our Lady of the Assassins,* 2000), who took advantage of the lightness of the digital camera to shoot in dangerous locations in Colombia; Pascal Arnold and Jean-Marc Barr (*Lovers* in 1999, *Too Much Flesh* and *Being Light* in 2001); and Pitof (*Vidocq* in 2001). And soon films that *don't* use digital special effects and digital cameras will be the exception rather than the rule.

The next step is the move to high-definition digital cameras. Daniel Langlois and his company Media Principia, which he founded in 1998, produced *The Baroness and the Pig,* written and directed by Michael Mackenzie and shot entirely in high-definition digital. He wanted to show that digital technology has progressed to the point that it is now indistinguishable from analogue, including when virtual sets are used. Digital technology has become invisible. Langlois didn't use a science fiction setting for his demonstration, as George Lucas does; instead he chose a story set in 19th-century Europe. Post-production was done entirely in Ex-Centris's studios in Montreal. In 2001, George Lucas insisted on shooting *Star Wars, Episode 2: Attack of the Clones* with an HD 24P digital camera. It was a manifesto in support of end-to-end digital, even though in 2002 he could screen his film digitally in only 23 theatres in the U.S. And then came Hollywood features produced using high-definition digital technology, often animated features and invariably with special effects, such as *Finding Nemo* (2002) produced by Pixar and distributed by Buena Vista; *Sinbad, Legend of the Seven Seas* (2002) directed by Tim Johnson; Jonathan Mostow's *Terminator 3* (2002);

Gore Verbinski's *Pirates of the Caribbean: The Curse of the Black Pearl* (2002), and others.

Digital Takes Hold

With the end of celluloid, the savings begin as early as the first stages of production. Not only is using a digital camera much cheaper than using a 35 mm camera, but recording on digital media means that filmmakers can see dailies right away on DVD, with much greater security than on a video assist device. Filmmakers can erase and re-record over and over on the same hard disk, significantly reducing the cost of shooting through the savings on film and lab expenses, but also by saving time. Given that digital technology is much more sensitive than silver emulsion film, movies can be shot in natural light, dispensing with heavy artificial lighting equipment. And the range of cameras on the market in terms of weight, sophistication, and price is always growing.

Many of today's documentaries and art and experimental films could not have been produced without digital technology. Films that don't have million-dollar budgets can now be made and produced in high definition. Post-production is already digital anyway, but digital distribution would eliminate the costs of transferring from celluloid to digital before editing and vice versa.

With an HD or video camera, shooting can take place in very difficult conditions where traditional equipment just can't go—for example, in battle zones, in areas that are dangerous due to guerrilla fighting or natural disasters, even in situations that require complete discretion, like in Afghanistan during the reign of the Taliban or in places that are officially off-limits. Plus, HD digital cameras can run on battery for close to 50 minutes, compared to 11 minutes with a 35 mm magazine, making it possible to follow the action without having to stop to recharge the camera. When making *Bowling for Columbine* and *Fahrenheit 9/11*, Michael Moore demonstrated that he was able to shoot using a pen camera without his subject knowing. The images may have been low-definition, but they were laden with meaning.

Footage can be shot in real time and immediately sent via satellite to a television station, a technique that can be ideal for documentaries and news reports. Using digital technology, the internet can even bypass and scoop major media.

Generally speaking, there are tremendous advantages to digital distribution. Blowing images up to 35 mm and producing prints is expensive and risky for the distributor. And then there are the expenses for managing reels: handling, cleaning, repair, and even destruction. American blockbusters can have several million 35 mm prints available for their opening; independent film producers often don't have the budget for a hundred, or even twenty, prints, which means that these films can't open in major theatres, relegating them to art and experimental theatres outside of urban multiplexes. Their potential for success is therefore limited from the outset. Digital copies and transmission by satellite would put an end to this seemingly insurmountable handicap. Additional copies could be produced without delay and their numbers could be adjusted daily. Digital distribution via satellite or high-speed internet is affordable, and the quality is equal to that of a master print. Plus simultaneous distribution to many theatres would cease to be a problem and would involve no additional costs, even over great distances.

When Hollywood distributors understand that they can launch a film simultaneously in 3,000 theatres, distributed via satellite for a pittance, and save $9–10 million at the outset, they're going to give the matter some serious thought.

Initial experiments in digital distribution included George Lucas's *Star Wars, Episode 1: The Phantom Menace* (1999) which played in 4 theatres in the U.S., followed by *Episode 2: Attack of the Clones* (2002), which was distributed to 94 theatres worldwide. John Lasseter's animated *Toy Story 2* and Walt Disney's *Fantasia 2000* were both screened digitally at the Gaumont Aquaboulevard theatre in Paris.

In Montreal in 1999, Daniel Langlois founded Ex-Centris, a digital theatre with several screens that successfully presents auteur films, which are generally excluded from the Hollywood movie circuit. Claude Chamberlan, the founder of Montreal's festival for new trends in film—the Festival international du nouveau cinema—is in charge of programming. Daniel Langlois has also designed Ex-Centris as a digital production and post-production centre and testing and research laboratory.

He is clear about his vision. For him, "digital technologies ... are important creative tools, but they're even more important as a means of distribution for independent cinema." He says, "My personal drive is independent film, not Hollywood cinema, and the only way to create a network to have access to cinemas from around the world will be by separating productions from the present distribution network. The only way to do that—because the costs of 35-mm prints are so high—will be by delivering films either by satellite or by land by digital means." And he adds, on a more personal note, "I try to bust through all hegemony. That's one of my main motives."[27]

To pursue this objective, he founded Pixnet, a company that distributes films via satellite. Pixnet is already distributing commercial documentaries and is getting ready to distribute features via satellite. He also heads up DigiScreen, a company that has developed an integrated digital compression, presentation, and management system for distributing films on digital media over landlines and projecting films digitally in theatres.

Daniel Langlois has since bought and re-equipped other theatres in Montreal, such as the Cinéma du Parc,[28] and all signs point to him expanding his network.

In Quebec City, the Cinéma Cartier, a 120-seat theatre equipped with DigiScreen technology and DVD, shows movies you can't find anywhere else, like Juan José Campanella's *Son of the Bride*, a Spanish-Argentinian co-production, screened for the theatre's opening in 2003, or Carlos Saura's *Goya in Bordeaux*, and retrospectives of auteur film. The man behind the independent theatre is the owner of a video club in the same building, Michel Savoy: "I have been living off video for twenty years. But for me, nothing replaces the collective experience of the movie theatre. This project may be a bit crazy, but I love film too much not to have tried. Ten years from now, we'll be seen as the pioneers."[29] This type of programming is so rare that the Régie du cinéma du Québec, the Quebec body that governs film, had to give the theatre permanent film festival status to allow it to present films without a visa. This sort of case will no doubt become more common and will result in changes to the regulations for film visas.

In 2002, Famous Players started to test digital projection in two theatres in Canada, at the Colossus in Woodbridge, Ontario and in Richmond, British Columbia. In 2002, other theatres opened: two in Vancouver, one in Toronto, one in Kitchener, and two NFB theatres.

In Toronto, filmmakers Atom Egoyan and Ron Mann, working with Hussain Amarshi, president of the distribution company Mongrel Media, decided to open an independent theatre equipped with digital projection technology.

The National Association of Theater Owners (NATO) in the U.S. makes a distinction between d-cinema, or digital film, which refers to very high resolution of 3K or 4K, and e-cinema, or electronic cinema, which refers to lower-resolution, standard 1K projections, including ads and teleconferences.

HD, as defined and adopted for television in 1999— HDTV—refers to the SMPTE standard of 1920 x 1080 pixels. In reality, HD is more commonly in the order of 1280 x 1024 pixels, what is referred to as 1K. In fact, a properly adjusted digital image of 1280 lines offers definition that is comparable to that of a standard 35 mm print, which is in the order of 1920 x 1080 pixels. With 2K, which corresponds to 1280 or 1536 x 2048 pixels, there is no room left for doubt. And 4K, 3072 x 4096 pixels or 4046 x 2048 pixels, corresponds to super 35 mm or 70 mm. Of course, the definition of 35 mm can be bumped up (granularity of silver on celluloid and sharpness of the angle of the shot with projection up to 5,000 digital lines), which corresponds to 4K. But what is to be gained, when 35 mm films currently go through digital formats in post-production and are only boosted, or kinescoped, to 35 mm at the very end of the process? They have already lost the original resolution of film recording, and nobody's complaining! Besides, the grading of colours, which traditionalists see as the determining factor in the quality of film, is already performed digitally more and more often.

Regardless, isn't it better to watch a master quality 1K digital image than a 35 mm image that is scratched, covered with awkwardly placed, persistent dust particles, and has already been around the block? In 2000, Mark Gill, president of Miramax Films, a Walt Disney group property, said, "For moviegoers, this is the start of a massive quality improvement: the end of torn film, fading, and scratches, and the beginning of true digital projection, where the last screening of a movie looks as good as the first."[30] Even Eastman Kodak, the symbol of celluloid silver emulsion film since the beginning of cinema, mindful of the competition to come, has headed down this road. Many experts point out that in fact a high-definition digital image is more luminous than the film-based image, more saturated and detailed, and most importantly, more stable with more vivid colours.

According to journalist George Chamberlin of the *San Diego Daily Transcript*, in 2000, Kim Haile, general manager of Qualcomm Digital Media, maintained that "[d]igital cinema has been gaining strong momentum in recent years as the industry recognizes that technology offers alternative means to reproduce and distribute entertainment products while extending the quality of the product for the consumer."[31]

George Lucas has come down publicly on the side of digital projection on many occasions: "With digital projection, it's so much easier to [ensure print quality], because the image won't degrade the way film does. The degradation of film for release prints is a constant battle filmmakers deal with. Film actually collapses if it plays constantly in a theater for two or three months. It's hard to even recognize what you are seeing after all that time. And if you let it sit two or three years, the color goes out. It looks terrible, even in some of the negative over time, and that makes it harder to restore it."[32] And digital technology is the only way to restore old films.

Here's an advantage not to be sniffed at: unlike 35 mm projectors, digital projectors do not have mechanisms that can make the image vibrate. A digital projector can be easily fine-tuned using a touch screen, and you can conduct quick tests to adapt a film to a screen, something that is unimaginable with an analogue projector. The 35 mm projector is a magnificent piece of machinery that hearkens back to the days of horse-drawn carriages, but it is completely obsolete in the digital era.

The Digital Distribution Revolution

In 1999, the American Secretary of Commerce estimated the annual cost of making and shipping prints of films at $750 million within the U.S. and $1.5 billion worldwide. This figure was confirmed by Viviane Reding, the European Commissioner for Education and Culture, at the Cannes Film Festival in 2002: "The move to digital cinema holds the promise of substantial savings for distributors, which could reach around 1.65 billion euros annually."[33] These tremendous sums of money would be better invested in production or in the quality of projection. And distributors could quickly become champions of digital distribution. For theatre owners, the problem is more complex.

There are inexpensive digital distribution technologies, like DVD, which is already the medium for many digital video cameras. However, its limited memory means using compression software for more professional applications, which hard disks are more appropriate for. However, the capacity of DVDs will increase quickly, given how entrenched this medium is becoming for other uses because of its ease of handling, affordability, and reliability. The Los Angeles Film Festival, for example, received 10% of its films on DVD in 1999, and 60% in 2001!

In developing countries, in particular in Brazil, some small theatre owners show films using DVDs bought in the U.S., in many cases without an exhibition licence. Sometimes this is the only way for these theatres to survive. If they were to stop their illegal activities, what would Hollywood gain? (The solution is actually in producing Brazilian films, once digital technology makes that possible.)

Microsoft, which systematically takes a position in any potential market, now wants to get into the movie business with the Windows Media 9 Series system, which can equip a small theatre. It includes high-quality sound and image, compression software specifically for film, combined with a small DLP projector, which provides perfectly acceptable projection quality from a compressed DVD. Certain theatre owners, like Landmark Theatres in the U.S., have shown an interest in this technology, which works for screens up to eight metres wide.

Microsoft is also offering Windows Media Player 9 Series for home theatres. And why not, although the market is somewhat limited. Film buffs have long had VHS tapes and sophisticated VCRs to record movies from TV when they're out of the house or asleep. And while technically VCRs work well, few people use them very often and more have forgotten how to program them. This is not to suggest that these aren't all excellent technologies, but their marketers have misunderstood how they are to be used. They have forgotten that cinema is a social art, and not just a technology.

DVDs are of course the most widely used medium for watching movies outside of theatres, replacing VHS cassettes, which had their moment of glory and memorable profits. For example, in Canada, recent estimates put box-office receipts at $450 million per year and revenue from VHS and DVD rentals at $1.5 billion. Home theatres generally operate on DVD.

Television, which devotes many hours of programming to movies and specialty movie channels, was accused of being behind the closure of theatres beginning in the 1960s, but it no longer seems to be a threat to the movie industry. On the contrary, it contributes substantially to revenues, because it has become the largest source of income in the exploitation chain of Hollywood movies since the creation of cable channels in the 1970s and pay-per-view in 1975. TV often plays a role in the production budgets of movies and always plays a role in their promotional campaigns, which is why the big seven have an interest in controlling television stations, following the well-established principle of commercial convergence.

We should be eternally grateful to television for letting us see old movies and documentaries during the decades when Hollywood's hegemony would have deprived us of these masterpieces.

Television has largely gone digital, whereas cinema has barely begun. And the convergence of HD DVD and HDTV is seeming more likely, which will make it possible to see a movie in HD DVD on TV. It won't be a revolution, but it will be better quality.

Clearly, VHS tapes don't create a movie experience and neither does DVD, even HD DVD; expensive home theatre equipment can't do it either. What makes the movie experience is the big screen and the collective ritual. When independent theatres reopen, including in small towns, home theatre will of course continue to exist, but the sale of films on DVD could plummet, countering the pessimistic forecasts of those who believe that DVD and home projection are tolling the bell for film.

The Pioneers of Digital Distribution

At the turn of the millennium, Daniel Langlois founded DigiScreen, which is based at Montreal's Ex-Centris. The company, managed by Pierre Latour, a former distributor of Film Tonic, and Mark Hooper, president and CTO, is trying to develop I-Cinema, meaning independent cinema, to break "the crushing grip of Hollywood, which has led the industry to the point that there are few places left to see other films, even in repertory theatres, which tend to show Hollywood movies after they have completed their first run."[34]

The company's prospectus is a virtual manifesto, sure to be of interest to movie lovers and defenders of auteur film! DigiScreen "proposes launching a network of independent theatres that will receive digitized films to present in medium capacity theatres with fewer than 200 seats." The company wants to offer theatre owners the digital projection technology, and give movie distributors access to a network using sophisticated management and distribution technology that allows them to create a repertoire of quality films likely to interest their audience. DigiScreen will therefore play the dual roles of telecommunications and programming: "To achieve its objectives, DigiScreen is currently coordinating the development of a low-cost, high-definition server, an efficient transmission network using satellites and physical media and process management software that will allow theatre owners and distributors to interact with the network via the internet."[35]

DigiScreen has also adopted compression, encoding, and decoding software, Elecard, which is Russian in origin and now being developed in Israel by Moonlight Cordless for PC and digital signal processor (DSP) platforms. Without getting into the obscure and soon-to-be obsolete technological details of the player, what it provides is rapid transfer and a high-quality image. The Elecard system already offers the H.264 standard, a derivative of MPEG-4, which makes it possible to quickly transfer a high-quality image at a low data rate, in the order of 100 to 500 KBps. That's more than enough for producing an image of sufficient quality that will be indistinguishable from traditional 35 mm film.

DigiScreen makes it possible to store up to 20 feature films, around 30 trailers, and ads on a 12-kilogram server no bigger than a PC. And DigiScreen offers something else of interest: you can ship up to a dozen feature films by bus to theatres equipped with their system, encoded on a hard drive in a case no larger than a standard video cassette. This makes it possible to deliver programming for a festival or a retrospective on a filmmaker in a lightweight format, without using cable or satellite, for a reasonable price. Besides, unlike 35 mm reels, the hard drive can be reused many times over for other programming, and it maintains its master quality.

A film technician can program screenings for a theatre using a touch screen that is as user-friendly as the point-of-sale systems found in restaurants, with an interface to control image and sound settings. The entire history of screenings would be stored in memory for managing the commercial aspects of distribution, and the encryption key would provide the distributor control over screenings and security against piracy.

While DigiScreen is pioneering with this technology by offering a complete, high-quality, low-cost system, these types of systems will obviously become more commonplace. Other technologies of the same sort are in development, including the reasonably priced Qube service from Real Image, an Indian company, and of course Microsoft's Windows Media 9 Series, which has already been tested in several dozen theatres in the U.S., but which doesn't tackle the problem of transmission.

At Ex-Centris's fifth anniversary in 2004, Daniel Langlois introduced DigiScreen as "the next leg of the journey in digital distribution, expanding the network without dramatically increasing marketing costs." "What interests us is diversity," he said. "The equipment would be leased for purchase in the form of a video server and film projector, for a total price tag of CAN$35,000, compared to the CAN$450,000 for equipment required by Hollywood to go to digital in its theatres. Theatre owners would recoup their investment in two years."[36]

And Langlois wants to license his system to other independent theatre networks, such as Digital Cinema Solution and Landmark in the United States, DocuZone in Europe, and the UK Film Council in Great Britain.

A number of other companies also offer digital film technology and have chosen to go with much higher-end systems, with much higher price tags, to placate the majors. Avica Technology specializes in digital post-production, distribution, and projection. It already demonstrated its abilities by delivering excellent digital distribution with its Digital Cinema Player technology at the 2004 Cannes Film Festival, screening the Spielberg-produced *Shrek 2*. The quality of the screening was hailed both by the public and by the president of France's Commission Supérieure Technique, Pierre William Glenn: "The quality of digital images is reaching a standard that now makes Digital Cinema a real alternative."[37] The company repeated the performance at the Cork Film Festival. The technology has already been used in the U.S., notably for a screening of the blockbuster *The Day After Tomorrow*.

Satellite appears to be the most promising means for digital film distribution, due to its power and wide footprint, which high-speed internet simply cannot compete with outside of major urban centres. Satellite also makes it possible to download feature films overnight to a digital server in theatres in outlying regions.

A number of companies are developing high-performance technologies for satellite distribution of movies. California's AccessIT has claimed to have had its d-cinema satellite delivery system fully operational since June 2004, sending a digital signal via an internet data centre and equipment manufactured by Boeing Digital Cinema. It plans to start by bringing some 30 American theatres equipped with digital receivers and projectors and the Hollywood Software system on to the network. Another American company, Microspace Communications Corporation, which specializes in satellite distribution for Velocity multiusers, announced at the Digital Cinema Summit at NAB 2004 a first in 4K-compatible distribution with 4K or 2K projectors, meeting Hollywood's requirements of the Digital Cinema Initiatives. Every day, new companies, such as GDC Technology, are carving out a place for themselves in the market of servers and technologies for digital projection. The technologies on offer will become more varied and complete and offer higher performance, because the market exists for them, and clearly all of these companies will bring a lot of pressure to bear to move into the post-analogue-film era.

Pixnet, another of Daniel Langlois's companies, which is already testing its technology by screening promotional films in Canada, is in the running for this market. In 2002, Pixnet sent *The Baroness and the Pig* by satellite from Montreal to a digital projector at the Toronto Film Festival. The competition for satellite distribution equipment has only just begun, and obviously this is a strategic, and potentially very profitable, market.

We know now that online newspapers didn't hurt the regular newspaper market, and while the problem in the music industry is real and serious, it's largely due to the solitary nature of listening that music encourages. Film is a theatre art; it is not compatible with the internet or a 14-inch screen. In spite of what is often said and backed up by outrageous estimates, piracy of movies via the internet has no impact on audience numbers in theatres. Piracy can even keep the flame burning for cinema and encourage people to go see real movies in real theatres. Even once the majority of households will have high-speed, broadband internet, with 1 GHz of speed, 100 times faster than the internet today, movie lovers will still prefer going to theatres. And once theatres are connected to a broadband fibre-optic network to download their films, as the NFB did with CaNet and its online cinematheque, internet distribution will be as easy to control as satellite distribution, making illegal use unlikely. This of course presupposes digitally and commercially controlled professional technologies, which have nothing to do with the individual downloading condemned as illegal pirating. The only thing that would circulate on the internet would be the decryption authorization provided by the distributor and the audit of the number of projections, in other words, the management data. And it is even conceivable that one day, theatres will be able to receive high-resolution feature films in just one second via internet or satellite, so that there are always movies on the big screen and controls over their distribution.

It's hard to imagine movie lovers building theatres at home, as if they were oil emirs, and inviting the help or the neighbours to join them. If this ever happened, it would be a marginal practice that would not threaten the future of film. On the contrary, it could very well create new moviegoers!

At the turn of the century, in a euphoric wave of magical thinking about the development of digital technology, some thought that film via the internet was going to be the end of theatres, just as Peter Drucker announced that e-learning would close down schools and universities and that new uses would have to be found for the buildings. The idea is as baseless as the heralded triumph of e-books, which were supposed to conquer the world and plunge publishers of traditional books into bankruptcy. But a book is a book, a webpage is a webpage. And a film is a film.

There are plenty of internet film festivals, like the Festival international du film sur Internet (FIFI), held in Lille, France in 2003; the Yahoo! Internet Online Film Festival; and many others that come and go. These festivals are great. If they help promote low-budget auteur productions, it's hard to find fault with them. They have captured the interest of well-known filmmakers. And high-speed internet can handle very short features, which so far are mainly animated films like the 2001 hit *Park Wars*, short stories, or dramatic news reports shot with a digital camera.

Hollywood star Robert Redford, who has put some distance between himself and Tinseltown, the creator of the Sundance Film Festival in Park City, Utah, is very supportive of digital technology and even of the internet: "In years past, technology and the indie filmmaker seemed mutually exclusive in the sense that indie filmmakers were often disdainful of technology, or, as per their nature, more interested in the human aspects of narrative filmmaking. Technology will democratize film. There are alternative networks of distribution that are going to come on the horizon that are going to make filmmaking easier."[38] The Sundance Film Festival has created an internet section for short features, animated films, and new forms of artistic expression, and awards an audience prize as decided by online vote. The festival created this project with a number of partners, including Vancouver's Digital Film Group.

Canada's Independent Film Channel is an online theatre that customers with high-speed internet or satellite network access pay for. It has positioned itself as one of the most innovative film sites in the world. According to the schedule on its homepage, it shows eight features daily, for example: *Fargo*, *Leaving Las Vegas*, *Requiem for a Dream*, *American Psycho*, *Run Lola Run*, and *Cider House Rules*. It offers a magazine on independent film and a wide array of films available for order. It's like a pay-TV movie channel for computers, but with more choice and information.

But as an art form, personal film is different from mainstream movies. Personal film can have significant social or experimental interest and can launch the careers of the great filmmakers of tomorrow. It should be supported, but it has no direct bearing on the distribution industry. The internet can be very effective at promoting film, but it will never replace it. Film and the web can complement each other, as long as they remain distinct. A website can be an interesting companion to a film, providing additional information on the filmmaker, actors, soundtrack, story, its making, and more.

The internet has yet to decide on its calling when it comes to the arts. And when it comes to movies, its destiny is to promote feature films, not to encourage piracy, and above all to disseminate works of art of another sort, of a new genre, over a network, in particular interactive and animated films that are very different from the cinema we are familiar with. McLuhan said that we always start off wanting to put old content in new media: books, television, theatre, cinema ... Then we invent new content that makes the most of the qualities of new media. In terms of its use, audience, images, and writing, the web has yet to be invented.

Eugenio Zanettile's famous *Quantum Project*, a 31-minute, $3 million American production that deals with quantum reality, will go down in the history of movies created for the internet as a noble, necessary experiment, but one that is totally marginal to the future of film, in spite of having been shown at the Cannes Film Festival. *The Blair Witch Project* (1999), co-produced by Eduardo Sánchez and Daniel Myrick, was such a hit that its website was paralysed by traffic when the movie was released. But that would have been its only claim to fame had it not had a second wind on video and DVD after grabbing attention at the Sundance Festival and being bought up by Artisan Entertainment for film and DVD distribution, who beat out Fine Line Features, Trimark Pictures, and Lions Gate Films for it. That's what's called hitting the big time; the film generated $140 million in box-office receipts. And if that's where dissemination on the internet can lead, so much the better!

Of course, the phenomenon of downloading music from the internet and the business model Apple adopted for i-Movie have got a lot of people thinking, and the majors are considering generating new revenue by tapping into their currently unproductive collection of repertory films, making them available on the internet for a modest payment, which could wind up bringing in big bucks. Of course, these are the same majors who have rejected digital distribution in the name of the quality of 35 mm film but who, suddenly, have forgotten this sacrosanct requirement, envisioning distribution of the lowest quality imaginable via the internet on a computer screen. The only thing these two contradictory positions have in common is profit, which is really what Hollywood is about.

In 2001, Metro-Goldwyn-Mayer, Viacom-Paramount, Vivendi Universal, and Warner Bros announced their intention to use

Sony's MovieFly platform to offer pay movies over the internet, soon followed by Twentieth Century Fox and Walt Disney/ Miramax. The battle had begun. Lion's Gate Entertainment launched CinemaNow.com, and the Blockbuster Entertainment Group also made the commitment to sell videos over the internet. Is anyone still talking about this "sure thing" Hollywood announced five years ago? It currently takes hours to download a movie, which is something of a disincentive, and the result is not much more encouraging.

The dissemination of movies via the internet won't be the golden egg that the majors are dreaming of, because the internet and computer screens are incompatible with film. On the other hand, as we saw with *You've Got Mail*, *The Matrix*, *The Net*, *Hackers*, and other movies, the web is a great source of material!

The Great Illusion of Film/Video Games

So why not create film/video games? Over multiuser networks? *The Matrix* set the example with the second and third parts in its trilogy, *The Matrix Reloaded* and *The Matrix Revolutions*, which looked more like video games than movies, the goal of which was undoubtedly to exploit the first film in the series, *The Matrix*, as a DVD game by taking advantage of the theatre release. The strategy failed. The reason for this effort was that DVDs of blockbusters often bring in more than the box office. Generally speaking, gamers maintain that video games based on Hollywood hits are usually flops.

Another current trend is the rapprochement between film, which is becoming more interactive, and games, which well-known filmmakers are being asked to develop. As a result, two major entertainment industries, cinema and gaming, are converging because of the spread of digital technology.

Hollywood's interest in gaming is easy to understand given that worldwide sales in the video game industry now surpass those of film. Copying the successful model of multiuser games, Hollywood could create interactive films played over a network. It would be nice if the artistic quality of games would improve, but this bold vision is hardly likely to revolutionize the film industry. Not everything can converge, and so much the better, both for movie lovers and gamers. A movie is a movie. A game is a game. The fact that all forms of communication are going digital does not mean that soon there will be a single digital art that encompasses music, literature, television, film, games, and dance! What a shame that would be.

The Digital Aesthetic

Digital technology clears the path for filmmakers to explore new aesthetics. Computer-generated special effects and the flexibility of editing provide a new connection with the incredible alchemy of Georges Méliès. And the lightness of the HD camera makes it possible to create a more natural documentary.

It is in this second sense that Lars von Trier became champion of a new aesthetic, adopted by the group Dogma 95, which has earned quite a following. The young Danish filmmakers in this group insist on unconventional shoots with light cameras and no lighting or artificial background sound. The technical and financial simplicity of such shoots verges on the austere, making poverty a virtue and an art, but the simplicity can also be frustrating (von Trier has referred to it as a cinematographic chastity belt). However, it doesn't change the fact that this sober approach results in an intense reality on-screen. This new aesthetic is the antithesis to the strict constraints of shooting in 35 mm, and is one of the new avenues that digital technology provides, of particular interest to filmmakers in developing countries where the intensity of the social documentary often prevails over aesthetic artifice. In general, filmmakers agree that digital technology is not only cheaper, but that it also offers much greater creative freedom and liberty in shooting. A lighter camera provides greater flexibility in the angle of the shot. Filmmakers have access to an on-site lab, even when they are shooting outside, so that they can immediately adjust lighting and acting. Being able to view the result immediately saves time and makes it possible to reshoot many times over.

Pitof, who made *Vidocq* in 2001, explains that his decision to use a digital camera was a technical one (the camera is much lighter), but that it was also an artistic choice, because the visual output came close to that of painting and made the story more mysterious. Peter Greenaway, another filmmaker for whom film resembles painting, also points to the creative power of digital technology. For such filmmakers, digital technology does not merely replace film for capturing images. The logic of the technology goes much deeper and takes them directly from the shoot to the editing table, where they can use a computer to transform shots without limit, the only constraint being creativity. Post-production becomes as important as shooting in making a film, perhaps even more decisive. Colours, contrast, the definition and the contour of a character or a background object can be reworked, adding an aura or melting it into the background, dramatizing an expression, reworking a line, editing in, cutting, repeating, and so forth. Editing, it is often said, can make or break a filmmaker's work, and filmmakers put themselves in the hands of the editing team. But now filmmakers have as much power in post-production as in shooting, which only provides the raw material for the studio, where they must be as involved as they were on the set.

With digital film, the real and the virtual combine to create hybrid cinema, offering new possibilities of expression. With special effects and much easier digital editing, filmmakers can use more fragmented space-times, faster rhythms, and a more dynamic style, to the point that some abuse it and create a zapping effect with their editing! This is no doubt the result of the acceleration of time, which film is echoing. The slow rhythm of films like Alain Resnais's *Hiroshima, mon amour* or *Last Year at Marienbad* seems a distant memory. George Lucas confirms this, "The reason ILM [Industrial Light and Magic] got started was because, [back during the making of the original *Star Wars*], I wanted to make a space opera that was very fast, very cinematic, with short cuts, lots of movement, very kinetic. I wanted to do it cinematic style, and the truth was, there was no way [technically] to do it."[39] Lucas does not seem interested in digital technology as a technology that will revolutionize distribution and the film market and create a renaissance of independent productions, an idea that doesn't even seem to have crossed his mind. He is a full stakeholder in the studio system. His profound conviction for digital production and distribution technology is instead due to his search for power, performance, and the avant-garde of digital technology that he wants to identify with. He points to the enormous costs, rather than the financial advantages, "For me, digital effects are necessary to my craft—an enhancement to tell stories. Everything we did was driven by that goal—finding better ways to tell stories ... It's not really [a medium] for people looking to get rich."[40]

Of course, the cost of computer-generated images has plummeted, and special effects will become more affordable.

McLuhan said that film, both in its scroll-like shape and its script, belongs to the culture of the book. With digital technology, this will become less true, resulting in a new, yet-to-be-invented aesthetic, which could end up being closer to music, dance, or television. Of course, there are still those who prefer traditional film over digital technology, like Jean Rouch who said that video was the AIDS of film. They unjustly criticize digital technology for being less beautiful, less nuanced, and less graphical. But this is mainly a question of habit, generation, and appropriation of a new technology. Change creates resistance, some of it justified, some of it not, but generally more psychological than objective. Fewer than ten years from now, digital technology will have become invisible. We won't even think about it. Are any moviegoers still asking metaphysical questions about 35 mm reels or discussing the projector's lenses? The only time they think about these things is when they are subjected to the visual aggression of scratches and dust on the screen, or when the film breaks. Cinema is not celluloid. It's more and different than that: it is the artistic creativity that Hollywood no longer delivers.

NOTES

27. Isa Tousignant, "Grand Mishaps: Technology Patron Daniel Langlois on the Hits and Misses of the Digital Wonder of *The Baroness and the Pig*—Interview," *Take One*, March–May 2003.

28. The Cinéma du Parc closed its doors on August 2, 2006.

29. Luc Perreault, "Quand le cinéma chasse la vidéo," *La Presse*, May 23, 2004.

30. Barry Willis, "Multi-Industry Push into Digital Film Distribution," *Ultimate AV*, November 19, 2000, http://ultimateavmag.com/news/10870/.

31. George Chamberlin, "Don't Blame 'Grinch' for Lack of Joy in Movie-ville— Too Many Screens Mean Hard Times Ahead," *San Diego Daily Transcript*, November 24, 2000.

32. Michael Goldman, "The Lucas POV," *Millimeter*, March 1, 2004, http://preview.millimeter.com/mag/video_exclusive_lucas_pov/

33. Eric Chol, "Le numérique peine à faire son cinéma," *L'Express*, August 5, 2003.

34. DigiScreen press kit.

35. Ibid.

36. Ibid.

37. Avica Technology Corporation, "Digital Presentation of *Shrek 2* Wows Audiences in Cannes," news release, June 29. 2004, http://www.avicatech.com/press/6-29-2004.html

38. Duane Byrge, "Redford: Sundance Defines Itself," The Hollywood Reporter.com, January 19, 2004, http://www.hollywoodreporter.com/thr/film/article_display.jsp?vnu_content_id=2071976

39. Goldman, "The Lucas POV."

40. Ibid.

HOLLY WIRED, OR DESTINY

The threats to the empire are accumulating: the rise of digital technologies beyond Hollywood's control, the financial risks of an increasingly speculative industry and therefore one that is vulnerable to change, and the competition from the alternative distribution networks that digital technology will revive.

Hollywood Software, a company that develops management and anti-piracy software for the film industry, points to the trend that increasingly confronts the big seven: digital distribution. Obviously, the majors view the success and spread of open code software like Linux no more kindly than does Microsoft, nor do they like DVD players that operate on Linux and bypass protection mechanisms. The battle started in 2001 between the MPAA and the Electronic Frontier Foundation, which defends the freedom of web users.

Is it inevitable that the big seven migrate to digital networks? Is it possible without bringing down the empire? The question for Hollywood is 2 be or not 2 be digital. The issue goes well beyond tracking illegal downloads on the internet, the MPAA's current obsession. It's a question of deciding whether or not the industry will abandon the 35 mm reel and go digital.

Irrespective of Hollywood's will to power, the first jolts to the empire came in the form of the enormous budgets the majors have needed to maintain their position and weather the financial and other crises they have had to endure. The financial need resulted in a speculative game of mergers and acquisitions, controlled by financial holding companies dominated by other companies and industries, such as Coca-Cola; the oil industry; Bronfman's spirits; Japanese companies including Sony, Matsuhita, and Toshiba; Australian companies, one in particular led by media baron Rupert Murdoch; and even European companies, for instance during Vivendi Universal's brief moment of glory.

If we analyze the origin and the ownership of capital that controls these major holding companies, we see that Hollywood is now the symbol of a conglomerate, which, like any self-respecting multinational, extends well beyond American borders; as a result, the industry's fellowship could easily start to fall apart.

Sony, one of the majors, is first and foremost a Japanese electronics company, but it also sells digital movie projectors—a market it certainly doesn't want to hand over to other manufacturers, given the current competition for digital equipment. But there's nothing stopping Sony from blazing a trail in Hollywood and supporting digital cinema, to ensure that it grabs a share of the market before the others. It wouldn't be the first time that a defection has occurred among the big seven. At a certain point, the MPAA could no longer ignore the digital alternative to 35 mm reels, and it decided to confront the problem.

When Hollywood Tried to Block Digital Technology

In 2000, the DC28 working group of the Digital Cinema Initiatives published its vision of the future of digital film: it would require a very high standard—4K—in order to agree to give up reels and move to digital projection, even though 2K, and even 1K, is the equivalent of film to the audience's eye, minus the scratches and dust.

According to the DCI, for a digital system to become the norm, it would need to respect the following conditions:

- It should significantly increase the opportunities for screenings.
- Its quality should surpass the quality of a 35 mm theatrical screening print.
- The system should allow for worldwide compatibility so as not to limit opportunities for distributing content.
- The components of the system should be standardized so that equipment from different suppliers is interconnectable.
- Equipment must be updateable to keep pace with advances in technology.
- The system must guarantee secure transmission over electronic routes (satellite, for example) and on physical media (DVD-ROM, for example). Security should be provided by an access code and electronic rights management made possible. Players should use online authentication so that content is never available unscrambled.
- The cost to purchase and use the equipment should be reasonable.

Hollywood understandably does not want to adopt a standard that would require theatres to pay ongoing royalties for screenings, as is the case with the Dolby Stereo sound system monopoly. Hollywood wants to establish its own standard, one that it controls or that works on a number of platforms, opening up competition and driving prices down. These are simple, common sense conditions in many respects, but they veil the strategic hold that the DC28 wants to impose, in the name of excellence, and in the form of the both useless and extremely expensive 4K standard for digital image definition.

In fact, 4K, or 2000 x 4000, does not work with any type of projector currently available on the market and is way ahead of standards for projectors, which barely go beyond 2K. It will likely be years before equipment manufacturers put out 4K projectors. Their price tag—around $350,000—will limit demand. Hollywood would have to make do with 2K projectors, even if it insists on 4K images.

The second roadblock is that with the current state of technology, the 4K standard would require four seconds per frame, or 250 hours to download a full-length feature. The professionals cannot ignore this fact. And this is where the hidden agenda of Hollywood's seemingly visceral opposition to digital distribution, in the name of excellence, becomes clear.

The MPAA clearly considers digital technology a Pandora's box that has to be handled with care, and, if possible, left shut altogether. The big seven want to parade their openness toward digital distribution publicly, but have chosen a standard that would delay its adoption for a very long time. Even if 4K projectors are developed someday, they would be out of reach for theatre owners, and 4K would require an extremely expensive film server.

The cynical beauty of Hollywood's strategy is to appear virtuous while theatre owners take the fall for resisting digital distribution, because they are the ones who have to assume the exorbitant expense of re-equipping their projection rooms with digital technology, while distributors are actually saving money. The MPAA has certainly cast itself in an enviable role.

As a result, a reasonably priced solution that offers sufficient quality to satisfy moviegoers needs to be targeted to exhibitors, who don't want to have to assume such high costs, particularly since many of them recently went into serious debt building multiplexes. Theatre owners all agree on this point. John Fithian, the president of the National Association of Theater Owners (NATO), pointed out in *Boxoffice Magazine* in 2003 that theatre owners unjustly came under too much pressure too early on to equip their theatres with digital projection, so they created a common front to avoid the excessive investment that it would require. But Fithian concluded that if general agreement could be reached regarding the quality required, a stable standard, and a reasonable price tag, he could change his mind, contingent on quality testing, as required by the Digital Cinema Initiatives, and theatres could start to use digital projectors as early as 2004. But to require, as NATO did, that the costs be shared with distributors is a completely unrealistic, and unlikely, solution. How would costs be shared among different distributors for a single theatre? It would be like handing American theatres over to distributors through long-term debt that would enslave them even further to one of the majors. Theatre owners would be virtually transformed into franchisees.

The big seven have the situation well in hand. And, in the mean time, 56 Hollywood films were parsimoniously screened using digital technology in 2003, a number of them only once, according to *The Hollywood Reporter*. The MPAA believes it has given itself enough time to get ready for what's coming. Plus, the Digital Cinema Initiatives' requirements date back to 2000, and they are no closer to being implemented, even though the H.264 standard is very promising.

On the other hand, in other countries where the 4K standard has not even been considered, and where governments are willing to subsidize theatres for the purchase of digital equipment to support their national film industry, the roadblock could quickly be cleared with the adoption of much more affordable 2K HD equipment. Logically, if this trend were to spread, American film could wind up cut off from the rest of the world, in a strange reversal of fortune. If Hollywood takes a hard line and manages to maintain its 4K requirement, the U.S. would continue to distribute film on 35 mm for its domestic market, but would have to offer digital versions of movies internationally.

As for the big players—Technicolor, Thomson, and Cinestore—they are trying to woo the MPAA by targeting the DC28 standard, but they will have to take another look at 2K or be drummed out of the market.

The Boogeyman: Digital Piracy

Even though piracy via the internet is not a serious threat to the film industry, Jack Valenti regularly gets up on his high horse to condemn the practice. He has created a boogeyman and accuses piracy of being at the root of significant losses in revenue, as is the case in the music industry. He has raised the staggering, dramatic figure of $3.5 billion in annual losses, allowing him to sidestep the issue of digital distribution, which would be a much bigger threat to Hollywood.

Valenti estimated that 350,000 movies are pirated every day worldwide via the internet. He points out that professional pirates have been found with up to 15,000 illegally downloaded films on their computers and that the MPAA sends more than 50,000 formal warnings of law suits each year to netizens (who are detected by the Ranger search engine). Obviously he is critical of sites that are the Napsters of the movies, such as Kazaa, Gnutella, Scour, iCrave, RecordTV, Morpheus, and Grokster.

In its fight against piracy, the MPAA has obtained the assistance of no less than the FBI, the United States Secret Service, the Department of Justice, and U.S. Customs and Border Protection.

Valenti himself has often said that cinema is a collective experience, a social event. It is not conducive to solitary viewing on a laptop screen. But the MPAA chooses to believe that piracy is a problem and is increasing the number of warnings issued and lawsuits. Valenti made piracy a major preoccupation in the final years of his presidency. And in 2003, the majors organized the Digital Media Summit in Universal City, in the heart of the Hollywood Hills, to discuss the issue.

The solemn joint statement (just the once can't hurt) of the president of the MPAA and the French minister of culture Jean-Jacques Aillagon against internet movie piracy at the Cannes Film Festival in June 2003 was touching: "Because valuable creative works of all countries deserve to be protected from digital thievery ... We urge the creative community and cinema professionals of France, the United States of America and all countries to join together in a common cause, indispensable to the future of every national cinema industry. That cause is the protection of films of every creed, culture and country. The world's cinema future is put to extreme peril ... "[41]

Similarly, Nicolas Seydoux, the president of both the film company Gaumont and a French anti-piracy association, the Association de lutte contre le piratage audiovisuel (ALPA), has been heard railing against the illegal downloading of films on the internet: "The phenomenon is very recent. Twelve months ago, the number of illegal downloads was still marginal. It was estimated at 30,000 per day in France. The Centre national de la cinématographie has just done a serious study of the question. The result: thanks to high-speed internet, there are suddenly a million illegal downloads per day in France. And this figure needs to be compared to the 500,000 daily admissions in theatres and the 200,000 DVDs sold every day. We have seen how the music industry was hit headlong by pirating—before it recovered this year. There is a mortal danger that is lying in wait for film today: if we don't do something now, we won't have 200 new films a year in

France; we'll have 25 every three years. And the first victims of this disaster will be new filmmakers and the most vulnerable parts of film industry."[42] Oh, the drama! But we must not confuse the pleasure of stealing without risk—which has become a national sport in many European countries, a form of resistance against the hegemony of large companies that grows out of the relationship between individualism and dominant commercial techno-structures—and use by movie lovers. From this perspective, movie piracy via the internet has no future. The act is simply a reflex against the excesses of globalization. In fact, French film is doing well: 200 new films this year is nothing to sneeze at. Five hundred thousand tickets sold per day is a lot. And 200,000 DVDs sold per day isn't bad either.

So why have Jack Valenti and Nicolas Seydoux suddenly put up barricades against the internet and not against illegal VHS copies, which have existed for decades, or DVD copies, which are a much more legitimate problem? This obsession with the internet is obviously the symptom of a much deeper fear, which has nothing to do with online piracy, a practice that remains anecdotal and that will soon be technically impossible; it does, however, have everything to do with the digital distribution of films, which will legally pluck the majors' sceptre of control over distribution from their hands. Bear in mind that Gaumont has signed agreements with Buena Vista, Walt Disney's distributor, and likely shares the same preoccupations about the future.

Downloading a Hollywood feature takes hours, even with high-speed access. Of course, it will soon be easier to do, given how quickly digital technology progresses. DivX is already on the market, a film compression software similar to what MP3 was for music piracy, because it divides the weight of a file by five and can reduce the time required to download a feature film from an entire night to just a few hours. But that's still a lot of effort compared to buying a DVD. So Jack Valenti went to war against Fast software, developed by the California Institute of Technology, which supposedly reduced the download time to a few seconds. But that's not where the problem lies. Until now, no DVD pirating has ever clearly threatened Hollywood's staggering profits, even when done by employees of the Oscar jury, the studios, or promotional companies; even when a film was put online before its release, as was the case for *Hulk. Hulk*, produced in 2003 by Universal Studios for $150 million, the onlining of which was fodder for the papers, still brought in $60 million in its first week, and several hundred million since!

In fact, according to a study by researchers at the University of Pennsylvania and AT&T Laboratories, Hollywood studio employees are behind most illegal onlinings of films. One study showed that 77% of films pirated between January 2002 and June 2003 were pirated from studio copies. "The majority of films (95%) were put online on peer-to-peer networks before their official release date in video stores, which means that the proportion of users who copy DVDs is for the time being marginal,"[43] the study said. The big seven would do better to monitor their own studios rather than throwing around accusations at internet users. Hollywood's battle against piracy, as blown up and dramatized by the MPAA, is based on exaggerated numbers that simply aren't credible, making the war suspect, at the very least.

Continuing with the same avowed obsession, the big seven have also spoken out against the danger of digital television, which could make it possible to record films and then circulate them on the internet. This shows that they don't understand the technology, because it would take extremely powerful professional compression software to make television files viable on the internet. Digital television signals require a throughput of 19.4 Mbits per second, which is unthinkable on the internet. And it also means attacking important market partners in distribution.

Hollywood points to the example of music, an industry that has actually suffered because of piracy. But music cannot be compared to film. Film is a collective ritual. Some music is as well, but most of it invites solitary listening, away from disruptions and noise. Film requires a large screen and high resolution, which the internet does not provide. And even in the case of music, in spite of such widespread piracy, and much praised internet radio, FM music stations have seen substantial increases in profits, at least in Canada for the past few years, with 15-year records in 2003–2004. Statistics Canada says that over the last six years, the profit margin of private radio broadcasters exceeded that of private television broadcasters. This points to two things: first, that media are unique, with the success of television taking nothing away from radio, which could, however, pass for a pint-sized version of a richer medium; second, that the internet has not hurt radio.

After an initial drop in ticket sales due to the rise of television in the 1950s, theatre admissions have been rising consistently for years. In the U.S., the number of screens virtually quadrupled between 1990 and 2004. The president of NATO himself pointed out that Americans are spending more time at the movies, putting money in the coffers of theatre owners.

Here are some official numbers (in billions):

	$	Tickets sold
1991	1.80	1.14
1997	6.22	1.36
1999	7.31	1.44
2001	8.13	1.43
2002	9.50	1.42

In Europe, theatre admissions have been consistently on the rise for the past several years, with 50 million more tickets sold in 1999 and 2000 (more than an 8% increase in France), and the momentum continues.

In Canada as well, audiences have been growing consistently for the past ten years. According to Statistics Canada, total admissions to theatres were 125.7 million in 2002–2003 (the country's population is only 32 million), or an increase of 5.4% over the previous year, in spite of the closing of 284 theatres across the country. And operating revenues grew by 21.1%, to $1.3 billion, 69% of which was for ticket sales alone and 31% of which was for concession sales (which confirms that going to the movies is a social activity and not just a convenience). Obviously, film is growing in popularity.

So the question needs to be posed again: is the supposed threat of piracy going to upset or slow the trend toward digital technology? The answer is no: what television, video cassettes, and DVDs have been unable to do, internet piracy has even less of a chance of doing, given the effort required to pirate movies and the poor quality of the result. No more than legal, paid-for downloading via the internet, the e-movie, based on Apple's iPod model, is going to hurt theatre takings.

Canadian statistics in 2004 already showed that after a period of excitement, no doubt quelled by the fear of the cyberpolice, illegal music downloads have decreased dramatically. The same thing will soon happen in film, where the problem of piracy will return to being the more traditional and legitimate problem of illegal DVD copies. And, since you can't stop progress, digital movie files, like music files, whether on the internet, DVD, or CD, will soon be armed with a traceable electronic signature, a tag in an invisible, encrypted file for detecting illegal use online, possibly even destroying the recording. Powerful search engines, financed with huge sums of money for the fight against terrorism, will have no trouble making such detections, once the law authorizes it—

authorization which has not yet been obtained in Canada, where in 2004 the Supreme Court refused to condemn music piracy. When standard home computers are connected to the internet, like a digital Panopticon, they are completely open to investigation by determined professionals and to control through cookies, which even make it possible to remotely destroy illegal files on the hard drive of the delinquent computer, should lawmakers get ruthless one day. This is not computer fantasy: the technology exists and once it gets the legal green light, it will become more pervasive. There are already disposable DVDs on the market that self-destruct after playing once or after a few hours or a few days, depending on how they are programmed.

Will Hollywood wind up reaching an agreement with the download site Kazaa to offer movies for affordable legal download? What a strange twist of fate that would be. People around the world would have access to movies at a reasonable price, without putting theatres at risk. The viewing experience would be mediocre, and frustrating compared to the real thing, which would drive people to real theatres, thereby ensuring their livelihood. And so much the better, if it works. Sony, AOL Time Warner, and Vivendi Universal already got together in 2002 to create a site to sell films online at Movielink.com, but they were sued by Intertainer for anti-competitive behaviour; Intertainer sells videos online and Microsoft, Intel, Comcast, and Quest are among its shareholders.

The Financial Empire Weakened

There is a major threat facing Hollywood that will contribute to its downfall. The industry has become highly speculative: it bets on the uncertain success of films and keeps raising the stakes. The constantly rising production and promotional costs worry Jack Valenti, who calls the growing financial risk a cost tapeworm.

Hollywood takes a major risk with every blockbuster. And in the past few years, the stock of a number of theatre chains has repeatedly taken a beating. There are some 37,000 theatres in the U.S.; according to analysts, the market can only truly support around 28,000. Why are these major theatre chains in financial difficulty when both audiences and ticket prices are up? It's because they renovated or built multiplexes, in particular in the suburbs of major cities, and to do so they went heavily into debt. For companies like Carmine Cinemas, AMC Entertainment, Lowes Cineplex Entertainment, and Regal Cinemas, annual losses in 1999 were $19.9 million, $55.2 million, $51.4 million, and $88.6 million respectively, and there have been bankruptcies and buy-outs since.

Even though the price of tickets has generally increased worldwide in the past few years, it has not kept pace with the rise in production and promotional costs, which are spiralling dangerously beyond the confines of a realistic business plan.

To rein in these exorbitant budgets, American producers have gotten into the habit of shooting where production costs are lower than in California, whether in Florida, Texas, or in Canada and more remote countries (productions filmed outside the U.S. are called runaway productions), but this practice is threatening the jobs of California film workers, and so the MPAA has condemned it.

The paycheques doled out to stars have become a Damocles' sword over movie profitability. Julia Roberts can command around $20 million for a single production. Of course, stars sell the picture, but returns on investment are getting smaller, which can be fatal in the event of a flop (the math can only be done once the film is produced and released).

There is much at stake financially in releasing blockbusters virtually simultaneously worldwide. Hollywood wants the world market to be entirely under its control. But to rationally exploit a world market, it has had to invest in a zoning system, which has become so complex to administer on such a large scale that the big seven can no longer manage. The number of multizone DVD players is increasing, and there is free download software that cracks DVD locking mechanisms, so that the infernal spiral of the race against the zoning calendar is becoming illusory. This is why Hollywood has developed a new strategy, called "day and date," which is designed to release blockbusters faster around the world. But in doing so, Hollywood is jumping from the frying pan into the fire, because this strategy is increasingly expensive, financially risky, and virtually untenable. It involves producing thousands of 35 mm prints in advance and increasing promotional budgets, without even having first tested the movie on the American market, as Hollywood has always done before investing in foreign markets to avoid the major losses associated with a flop. The strategy is becoming a vicious circle, the negative effects of which are felt by its creators, and it is threatening the financial foundation of the edifice. All empires fall by virtue of wanting what is beyond their ability to control.

Jack Valenti himself has often pointed to the worrisome figures: given the major budgets for Hollywood films, estimates are that only 1.5 out of 10 turn a profit; of course these profits are so considerable that they make up for, and sometimes more than make up for, the losses of the other movies. Assuming that it's true that only 15% of movies turn a profit, then the Hollywood business model really is under attack by its very logic. If the big seven believe that this is the price they have to pay to control local and international markets, then Hollywood is on the road to ruin, digital distribution revolution aside. Sales are on the rise, but not profitability, exposing the majors to even greater risk. The Metro-Goldwyn-Mayer lion, so often seen roaring from the screen, is losing its teeth. In four years, MGM's sales increased by 52%, but it did not turn a profit once in those same four years. The slightest incident anywhere in the world could be

MGM's deathblow. So it has been put on the block. It won't be easy for production and distribution companies, who have developed lavish habits, to adapt to more modest, realistic business models, which they have forgotten how to manage. However, in 2006 Disney was forced to reduce the number of films it produces and distributes by around 25% and eliminate 650 jobs.

Hollywood is so vulnerable that Jack Valenti made a statement on April 23, 2003 to Congress on the serious threats to the future of American film, again raising the issue of the billions of dollars the industry is losing to illegal DVDs and piracy via the internet. The title of this statement leaves no room for interpretation: "A Clear Present and Future Danger: The Potential Undoing of America's Greatest Export Prize."[44] (The purpose of this statement was to dramatize the situation to obtain stronger legislative measures for the protection of intellectual property.)

The Digital War Has Begun

The war that is being waged is actually among digital equipment suppliers, who are going to fight tooth and nail to capture this strategic market and to win over the MPAA in spite of itself.

Thus, Kodak has been forced to change direction and has been carrying out a relentless promotional campaign to sell a 4K+ digital system worthy of the Kodak name to the majors. The company is offering a complete solution, including a server, a high-end projector, and sophisticated compression, encryption, and management software, which can be used for satellite or broadband cable. At the 2004 ShoWest in Las Vegas, the general manager of Kodak's Entertainment Imaging division, Robert Mayson, said that with the growing success of digital cinema, the company was positioning itself to lead in the new market. Mayson said that Kodak's objective was not just to offer a superior screen image; the company wanted to work with the profession to guarantee that its system would offer creative, technical, operational, and commercial advantages for all concerned. What more could you ask for, if you have the budget for it? And the price war has just begun. Kodak should count on going up against Dalsa, a Canadian company that is announcing more power, more options, and more creative control with its 4K Digital Intermediate Process. Kodak will also end up competing with France's Thomson, which has taken complete control from American Qualcomm over Technicolor Digital Cinema, and which is also offering turnkey solutions with software and equipment included. Since 2000, Qualcomm had already equipped close to 40 multiplex screens digitally for special events. The purpose here is not to give digital equipment companies exposure, nor to burden readers with too much technical detail. However, for several years now the largest companies, including Barco, Sony, Texas Instruments, Boeing Digital, JVC, Panasonic, NEC, Christie (Ontario), and Hughes, not to mention Microsoft, IBM, and others, have been announcing the launch of 2K digital projectors, each with higher performance than the last.

Several of these companies, in particular Texas Instruments and Dolby Laboratories (because the digital sound industry won't be outdone) got together to form the Digital Cinema Providers Group, which is trying to capture the projection equipment market. The group has already convinced Regal Entertainments, the largest theatre chain in the United States, and its subsidiary CineMedia to conduct testing.

In fact, another battle has begun to be waged against the big seven, whose conservative position on new technologies is starting to generate widespread disapproval in the digital technology industry. Major companies like Microsoft, Apple, Dell, IBM, and HP, as well as associations of consumers exasperated by the obsessive focus on piracy, have formed the Alliance for Digital Progress, the ADP. The ADP is fighting against the MPAA's lobbying to Congress for a law requiring producers of computer equipment (any kind of equipment or software that reproduces, posts, or accesses protected works) to include anti-piracy devices in their equipment. Both commercially and technically, such a law, now called the Hollings Bill after one of the Republicans supporting it in Congress, is obviously unthinkable. And yet, the MPAA is tirelessly pushing for it.

The Last Hollywood Battle for World Domination

Jack Valenti believes he is fighting a World War of Trade. What he is anticipating and is resisting with all the might and means of the MPAA is the rise of digital film. He is not resisting digital production, as long as in the end, after having produced a film using digital technology, from shooting to post-production, 35 mm reels are still used to distribute films, facilitating the control of theatres. What he is resisting is digital distribution.

Hollywood appears to be at the height of its glory and power. What a splendid, impregnable rampart! What a magnificent fortress of power and control worthy of Vauban! What a fantastic strategy for world domination and empire building, depending on which side you find yourself on, of course: on the inside, alongside the dominators, or on the outside, among the colonized.

The colonized, however, have the means of their liberation: first, to develop independent distribution networks, and then, to interest theatre owners in taking back control of their operations. Hollywood sees promoters of digital technology as barbarians who are threatening the empire, and without even invading its sacred hills, these barbarians will create a more promising alternative that will take hold gently ... with the gentleness of digital technology!

Because the battle in the film industry now hinges on distribution. Distribution on digital media, by satellite, and by broadband internet will end the big seven's hegemony over the distribution network. The 35 mm print has no future. For movie lovers, the 35 mm reel evokes the early days of the epic journey of film; what a shame that it has become a symbol of Hollywood imperialism. And when Hollywood loses control over theatres worldwide, it will also lose control over the DVD, pay-TV, and tie-in merchandise markets. It will lose the key to its kingdom, and it will have a hard time adapting to its shrinking markets. Hollywood will have the choice of folding or hopefully picking itself up again, taking its rightful and more modest place in the chorus of productions from around the world.

Hollywood is the perfect example of successful American globalization, tough in business and so cynical and powerful that its victims have often been consenting. Hollywood has been the wicked paradigm of globalization American-style, one that the U.S. would love to propagate. The big seven have won almost all of their battles, but they are going to lose the digital war, because the very forces of the digital realm are contrary to the MPAA's global control mechanism. And the war will play itself out fairly quickly.

It is true that Hollywood has reigned as tyrannically over the U.S. as it has over other countries. Its multiplexes have fed on independent theatres. Perhaps when the empire falls, we will discover a new America. Perhaps even Americans, who have become less likely to travel beyond their own borders, will soon have the chance to see foreign films in their theatres, opening their eyes to other cultures and other movie art forms.

The Late Hollywood Empire

Like all empires, Hollywood had a legendary beginning, a rise to power, and divinities enthroned on its famous hills, but it has also seen its share of conspiracies, its inside battles—fought hard—and of course the usual by-product of any great power: abuses, assassinations, and suicides. There is too much power, pride, and most of all, money for it to have escaped these ill effects.

Empire? Or saga? Regardless, the suspicious suicides of Marilyn Monroe and a few others became symbols, as did the grandeur and decadence of moguls like Mike Ovitz, who became president of Walt Disney in 1995 and who left, after a few bitter failures and some questionable speculation, with $109 million in severance pay and $120 million in stock options, which he discussed in an interview with the appropriately named *Vanity Fair*. Sometimes the knives fly under the radar in Hollywood, and the American dream can quickly turn into the American nightmare.

Fellowship among cartel members has its limits. Everyone is watching everyone else. What else can you expect when an empire starts to crumble? There is so much money at stake, such a fast rate of production and such large, regular financial risks that a tremor could turn into a financial earthquake, with a settling of scores worthy of the end of the Roman Empire.

There are empires that are stylish in their decadence, that encourage affectations, creative lavishness, inventive freedom, poignant tragedies, and memorable sensuality. This is hardly the case for Hollywood productions, which trot out hackneyed remakes, tired framing and heroes, and thin revenues, which even big budgets and star actors can't fatten. Being creative is too much of a risk with $200 million, and a billion dollars at the box office, at stake.

Jack Valenti's Retirement

Jack Valenti, who became president of the MPAA in 1966, is the symbol of the Hollywood system, which he personally wanted to incarnate. In spite of his legendary panache, even *his* optimism is not unshakable: he believes that with the rise of digital technology, the future will be bleak. And when a student asked him at the MIT Communications Forum in April 2004, "Can you elaborate on what a bleak future for the movie industry might actually look like?" he replied, "It won't be the end of Hollywood, but it will be very different. There will be more pilfering of movies, because it is so easy. There will be less investment in films, fewer films made, and jobs will be lost. There is already much unrest over movie productions moving to Canada, so imagine if there are fewer productions."[45]

The empire has become vulnerable, not so much because of "pilfering" but because of digital distribution, a perfectly legal practice and one that does not take place behind closed doors, which is going to give new life to independent distribution networks. These networks will initially exist alongside those of the MPAA, then they will grow stronger and compete with them, winning the favour of new producers who will find a new lease on life through these distribution channels, and soon they will threaten the profitability of Hollywood networks, possibly with internal complicity among the majors or from major filmmakers who want to regain their freedom from the all-powerful big seven. And because of its excesses, Hollywood is so financially vulnerable that the empire could fall faster than we think.

There is also a growing resistance to the system's hegemony that is organizing and spreading worldwide. The pendulum is swinging toward cultural diversity, which will shake the foundations of arrogant American globalization.

Of course, the big seven will likely try to buy up these independent distribution networks as they appear, either to kill them off or to swallow them whole into their own networks. But these burgeoning networks will likely pop up everywhere and will be too numerous to control. And history shows that empires, like walls, often crumble in a single block, as they grow too big and too inflexible to adapt to mounting external pressure.

Jack Valenti has retired, at the age of 82, after 38 years of lobbying at the head of the MPAA. And the announcement of his retirement, in 2004, may well have been the signal of the decline of the empire he presided over so arrogantly. With his departure, the curtain closes on the 20th century and the golden age of Hollywood. Dan Glickman is his successor. Is he a former actor? An experienced director or producer? No: he is a former elected representative of Kansas and minister of agriculture from 1995 to 2001. Perhaps it's a good choice for producing and marketing turkeys. Will he stay at the helm of the MPAA for several decades as Valenti did? He will have insurmountable challenges to face, and he will need to be philosophical to withstand the shaking of the empire and to remain on the deck of the *Titanic*, which has only seen the tip of the digital iceberg.

NOTES

41. *Cannes declaration*, May 17, 2003, http://www.culture.gouv.fr/culture/actualites/conferen/Aillagon2002/protectionfilms.htm#anglaise

42. Louis-Bernard Robitaille, "Alerte aux pirates! Le téléchargement de films explose: 1 million par jour en France," *La Presse*, "Arts et Spectacles," May 21, 2004, 2.

43. Christophe Guillemin, "La majorité des films pirates sur le net sort directement des studios d'Hollywood," *ZDNet France*, September 19, 2003, http://www.zdnet.fr/actualites/internet/0,39020774,39124124,00.htm

44. MPAA, "A Clear Present and Future Danger: The Potential Undoing of America's Greatest Export Trade Prize," news release, April 23, 2002.

45. "Movies in the Digital Age."

The Digital Flood

The digital revolution will happen in less than a decade. The technology is ready, the standards will start to stabilize, and the business models will become convincing for theatre owners, distributors, and producers, to the great advantage of the independents.

Where Are We in 2004?

There are an estimated 2,000 theatres worldwide equipped with digital projectors, and there will probably be 5,000 by the end of 2005, including electronic movie theatres. Their numbers are expected to grow exponentially, strengthening the business model for this type of distribution. Once theatre owners start saving on the significant expense of creating and transporting 35 mm prints, and once they have regained virtually unlimited freedom, richness, and flexibility of programming, theatres, including those in small towns and remote regions, will see a new profitability that will make their numbers grow.

The first theatres to be digitally equipped will likely be those with fewer than 200 seats, i.e. repertory, art, and experimental theatres. Many of these theatres are in difficulty, admissions are limited, and they are in danger of closing. Their continued operation in no way threatens Hollywood, for the time being.

But once these theatres start to see the profits that digital technology will generate and offer a greater selection of movies as a result, the movement could take hold and encourage owners of busier independent theatres to move to the new technology as well, particularly if they can do so at a reasonable cost. Then, competition with networks that are currently controlled by Hollywood distributors will heat up. In an industry driven by profit, the appeal of digital distribution and projection systems will grow quickly. Multiplexes will be able to try digital projectors out in one theatre, then two, then three ... without getting rid of 35 mm projectors right away.

Companies like NovoCiné, which was created in 2001, have announced that they want to help theatre operators in the move to digital cinema by offering mixed transitional technologies that make digital servers and projectors compatible with 35 mm reels.

Outlying areas are often veritable movie deserts. Quebec proudly points to the Festival de Rouyn-Noranda, which each year offers audiences far away from Montreal and Quebec City quality programming. An alternative film association in Quebec, the Association des cinemas parallèles, has made some remarkable efforts. But the results are uneven, as is the case throughout Canada.

Even in the U.S., the situation is starting to improve. In 2003, Landmark Theatres, a distributor of art and experimental film, decided to equip 177 screens in 53 theatres in 13 states with digital projectors. There are already a number of digital theatre networks in the U.S., in particular those belonging to the AMC and Loews groups, with 20 screens in total. Companies that sell digital equipment and services are trying to increase the number of special events, for example digital film launches, to promote their expertise and win over the majors. Of course, in spite of being competitors, the majors have always presented a united front against digital distribution. Only LucasFilm and

Walt Disney are relatively open to it, no doubt because the former produces science fiction movies that increasingly use computer-generated special effects and that are now wholly produced digitally, and the latter has a long tradition of animation, which is now also produced entirely by computer. It's ironic that the country with the most developed digital technology industries, where conditions are perfect to adapt digital technology to movie distribution, is the country that resists it the most, with the MPAA leading the charge. It's an irony that is weakening the Hollywood fortress.

Things are moving a lot faster in Europe. As of 2002, the European Commission, in a meeting in Seville presided over by Spain, invited the European film industry to adopt digital technology: "The transfer from 35 mm film to digital cinema should occur in the best possible way and achieving the best benefits to all users. To ensure that the exhibition industry and the distribution industry move in this direction, an awareness action, supported by the European Commission and government bodies, should widely explain the benefits of such a change. The transfer from 35 mm film to digital cinema has to provide real benefits to all parties in the cinema value chain, filmmakers, studios, distributors, exhibitors, and theatre audiences. In order for these benefits to be effective, further and detailed inputs from representatives of all actors are necessary:

"Within this process, the exhibition sector needs to be considered carefully as it constitutes the very important place for showing of film/event. Digital cinema requires a minimum users requirements for theatrical exhibition: similar quality to 35 mm, standardized systems and interoperability of equipment, secure content transport mechanisms, conditional access for projection material, copyright protection, security needs to be implemented so as to protect the rights and copyright of content owners as well as the necessary flexibility and autonomy of the exhibitor, and reasonable costs.

"Government incentives should favour this process of gradual introduction of quality digital, especially in rural or low income areas.

"In this sense the works developed by the European Digital Forum with the support of the European Commission, as well as other initiatives of the European Commission for the introduction of digital technology such as MEDIA Plus (pilot projects) and 'i2i Audiovisual' are especially important."[46]

The European Space Agency (ESA) has developed a project called E-Screen to implement a network for distributing digital film via satellite across Europe. In 2003, this project had already been test driven in seven theatres in five European countries. A meeting of specialists and industry partners debated the issue in August 2003 at the 60th Venice Film Festival, and of course the debates were transmitted by satellite to European ministers who will decide on the issue. Claudio Mastracci, the director of the ESA project, pointed out, "Once again ESA ... is promoting the development of new applications ... in the multimedia satellite market, which is led by the growth in demand for innovative services such as High-Definition TV and Digital and Electronic Cinema, soon to become a reality in Europe."[47]

The tone of this statement of principles, intended to inspire film policies of member governments, seems much more visionary, and at the same time more realistic, than the statement of Hollywood's Digital Cinema Initiatives, which demanded the impossible.

In 2003, the European Union's MEDIA Plus program decided to finance 40% of the cost of the equipment in 11 digital theatres as part of an initial test, and entrusted the implementation of this project, called D-Cinema Europa

Network (DCEN), to a European agency that promotes digital cinema, the Agence européenne pour le développement du cinéma numérique (ADN). The objective of the ADN, which was founded in 2000 to promote and use digital technology for d-cinema in European theatres, is to support the transformation in the film sector in order to improve the circulation of European films within Europe and to increase audiences.

The ADN wants to demonstrate that digital distribution will make it technically and economically more efficient to distribute feature films in Europe than using 35 mm reels, with the same quality of projection.

In Great Britain, where Hollywood movies currently account for 90% of screen time, the UK Film Council, financed by lotteries that inject £50 million annually into British film production and distribution, committed to creating 250 digital theatres by 2005. Richard Morris, who joined the UK Film Council as part of the Digital Screen Network, stated, "It will dramatically alter the landscape. The whole idea is to make independent film more accessible to everyone."[48]

"What we want from a film perspective is more diversity and a wider range of specialized films," he said during a 2003 conference on e-cinema organized by the NFB in Montreal. "When I say 'specialized films,' I'm talking about independent, foreign and British films. We want to widen the programming of mainstream cinemas. As we all know, most multiplexes around the world are studio orientated, full of American content. And that's not enough. There's a huge demographic who demand to see and deserve to see alternative product and alternative films. So we want to increase audience appreciation of film, as much as a cultural and an entertainment offer. There's so much more to see in the world than what studios have to offer."[49]

In 2004, the director of the UK Film Council, John Woodward, pointed out that digital film distribution requires public funding, because private companies believe that the economic risks are still too high. And Paul Kafno, president and CEO of HD Thames, got into the development of electronic theatres, in particular to disseminate what he calls electronic theatre to outlying areas, because this art form is very highly valued in Great Britain, but obviously not very accessible outside of major cities.

Bill Nemtin, NFB delegate in Great Britain and someone who has been involved in Canadian film distribution, points out that digital will make it possible to produce new films that are likely to reach new target audiences because of the themes they address, and also new forms of cinema that are different from what we know today. He notes, however, that the development of digital cinema is still suffering from a lack of economic support, availability of films, promotion, and distribution infrastructures. Nemtin hopes that the transformation will shake up the Hollywood system by fragmenting its now-captive audiences through competition, and he believes that we have a window of maybe three years to successfully set up an alternative system of distribution, which presupposes quickly convincing public and private financial backers.

In the Netherlands, the Dutch Film Fund initially helped finance setting ten theatres up with electronic projection systems. And Kees Ryninks, head of the documentary section, in exchange obtained an agreement that the theatres would regularly show documentaries selected by the Fund, delivered on DVD. This launched the Thursday DocuZone documentary project. DocuZone has now spread throughout Europe and is subsidized by the MEDIA Plus program in Brussels, the goal of which is to support European film. The MEDIA Plus program decided to devote 5% of its annual budget to digital projection equipment for theatres. DocuZone is now active in Belgium, Scotland, Germany, Switzerland, Austria, Slovakia, Spain, and Portugal. And the number of theatres with digital equipment is on the rise: 25 more theatres in the Netherlands, 7 in Scotland, 7 in Belgium, 112 in Germany, 15 in Switzerland, 7 in Austria, and there are theatres going digital in other countries. In Germany, the federal government decided to assume 50% of the costs of the project to speed it up. During a 2003 conference organized by the NFB and the Festival du nouveau cinéma in Montreal, Kees Ryninks said, "How can we protect our European film culture against the incredible influx of American titles? One of the things I think is the most exciting part of setting up this network is that it will be easy to exchange programming. What is nice about it is that the satellite-based system allows for live events, where a director can introduce his or her film live to the 175 cinemas, and afterwards we can do Q&A's. The reason for doing that is that one of the things we noticed in Holland was that when the director was present at the Q&A, our audience figures doubled. It's very important to create an event of each showing, and because it's satellite-based there is the opportunity to do that, to make it something exciting."[50]

And Ryninks also pointed out that these networks will promote the exchange of films as well as co-productions. At the Nyon Film Festival in 2004, he reaffirmed it, "Digital distribution is spreading like wildfire around the world."[51]

In 2004 in Belgium, the Kinepolis Group already had ten theatres equipped with digital technology in Brussels, Antwerp, Liège, Ghent, Hasselt, Kortrijk, Leuven, and Braine-l'Alleud. Kinepolis has adopted the 2K standard.

In France, a professional audiovisual association, the Commission supérieure technique de l'image et du son, which plays a major role in the film industry, increased the number of working conferences on this key issue. There is also the European Digital Cinema Forum (EDCF), which brings together all the players in digital cinema in Europe, from producers to exhibitors, and represents them in international forums on digital film standards; the first digital film forum was organized in 2003 in Monaco, the International Digital Film Forum (I-DIFF). And every year now the Cannes Festival welcomes digitally projected films, and debates the future of cinema and initiatives like Frederic Comtet's Digital Beach: "The Digital Beach concept is to create partnerships all along the digital chain: shooting, distribution, and screening. With digital technology, there is a true alternative to traditional distribution. This is why I'm currently working on feature projects in DV and why I've acquired an interest in NovoCiné, which is trying to set up an alternative network of theatres that screen films digitally, based on the Cinéma Utopia model from Bordeaux."[52] Aside from the Aquaboulevard theatre in Paris, there are already digital theatres in Lyon and Grenoble.

Latin American countries, which can't support powerful film industries but which are a major potential market for Latin culture, be it Spanish or Portuguese, can't help but benefit from digital technology, which will make it affordable to produce, distribute, and reach often scattered populations with a new Latin American cinema, using satellite distribution. Distances are long and transport often difficult and expensive, and as long as film has been distributed on 35 mm reels, Latin American countries have had one of the most sparse theatre networks in the world (1 theatre per 105,000 people in Brazil, 1 per 35,000 in Mexico, while in the U.S., a country with a much larger territory, the rate jumps to 1 theatre per 6,500 habitants). This is mainly due to the prohibitive cost of 35 mm prints and their transport and the climate's wear and tear on film.

This situation is going to change dramatically. Digital film is sure to succeed in Latin America, and it will spread quickly because Latin American audiences are potentially big movie lovers, which they now watch mainly on television if they are outside of the major urban centres where Hollywood multiplexes are located. Low-cost 1K distribution on DVD would work just as well for social and activist film as for fantasy films, which dominate Latin American film culture.

There have already been a few firsts. In October 2003, the Brazilian company Rain Networks, which offers reasonably priced digital film distribution, organized the screening of the Brazilian film *Os Normais* (literally, the normal ones) in São Paulo, attracting attention for the fact that this film was entirely digital, from production to projection, thanks to Rain Networks' KinoCast system and DRM software. "The public liked what they saw on the screen [and] the industry was comfortable with the knowledge that we had found solutions for piracy [and] distribution. It was a landmark for Brazilian cinema,"[53] the head of the festival pointed out. And the decision was made to set up a satellite network of 100 digital theatres by 2005 supported by Rain Networks from a server located in São Paulo, making Brazil a pioneer in digital film distribution.

Of course, among Brazilians there is a very high rate of connection to the internet. The country has widespread high-performance electronic banking, income tax filing, and voting systems. Brazil was also the first country in the world to develop a strong commercial DVD industry, when markets in developed countries were still stuck on VHS cassettes. The infrastructure exists, and could easily support the development of electronic cinema, either via DVD, or using the Windows Media Player 9 Series from Microsoft, which is targeting this market.

Film distributors in Latin America are therefore impatiently awaiting the arrival of digital distribution. Even the president of American-owned Cinemark Brazil, which has a network of 280 screens, is convinced that digital distribution is the new technological reality of cinema.

Cuba has managed to keep major film production alive in spite of the American embargo. The country also sustains an institute for art and film, the Instituto Cubano del Arte e Industria Cinematográficos, or ICAIC, and a number of dynamic film festivals that draw educated movie lovers, in particular the Festival Internacional del Nuevo Cine Latinamericano, headed by Alfredo Guevara. More than any other country, Cuba is pinning its hopes on digital technology to make it more affordable to produce and distribute Cuban and foreign films. "Cuba has succeeded in distributing films mainly through television, and now, with electronic cinema, using the high-speed Internet network that covers the entire island, with 350 electronic terminals," Omar Gonzalez, the president of the ICAIC said when interviewed in 2004. He points out that in 2003, Cuba produced 8 feature films, 17 short features, and 1 animated film, for a total of 26 productions—a lot for a small country: "And this rate of production will increase with the reduced cost of digital technology, which for us is essential."[54] Cultural diversity in film was deemed a priority issue for discussion during the 2007 Culture and Development Conference in Havana.

Digital technology, then, will spread like wildfire in Latin America. In Venezuela, Hollywood occupies 98% of the market, keeping out films from Europe and other continents; as a result, there is virtually no Venezuelan national cinema. Following the 2005 enactment of a law instituting a national film industry, the government decided to create an alternative to the de facto monopoly of American movie complexes. "We would like to oppose the cultural dictatorship of Hollywood, which forces productions on us that are foreign to our traditions," Venezuela's president Hugo Chavez said. "Hollywood portrays Latin Americans as violent criminals and drug dealers, and we want to offer young people role models other than Superman, for instance Francisco de

Miranda." And the minister of culture added, "Similarly, Indians are always portrayed as the bad guys in American films, as delinquents, killers, and terrorists." Venezuela therefore decided, as of 2006, to open a movie theatre with a digital projector in every state, for a total of 25 theatres, to show films on DVD. The country also inaugurated the Villa del Cine, covering five hectares of territory in Guarenas in the state of Miranda, to support the development of independent Venezuelan cinema. At a cost of 35 billion bolivars, the Villa del Cine will offer production and post-production studios, as well as a school for film studies and production. On the heels of the 2005 creation of the Venezuelan initiative teleSUR, a Latin American TV network broadcast in Spanish across the continent that could give the American CNN a run for its money, the project could quickly become a Latin American digital distribution network for independent film and programs with a social purpose. Wider access to satellite distribution, anticipated for 2007, will make such a network on a wide scale possible.

In Ecuador, Juan Carlos Tamayo has said, "Digital technology is the alternative that emerging countries were waiting for, and that increasingly directors and distributors are talking about. Digital cinema, or non-budget cinema, auteur cinema, or low budget cinema, has become the solution for those who want to make films. In recent years, there have been more films produced than in the entire history of Ecuador."[55]

Likewise in Chile, "something seems to be changing in Creole film production," as the online magazine *Chile.com* points out. "Up until now, film was considered an extremely expensive art form that required teams of professionals for a 35 mm production; the new technologies will change this way of seeing things by reducing costs dramatically, without compromising excellent quality."[56]

And activist film, which is very much alive in Latin America, has the potential for a second wind with digital technology. Filmmaker Boris Quercia, who directed Chile's first digital film, said, "*LSD* is a guerrilla film, which follows a march. The light digital camera made it possible to follow the actors and the action. Digital video is the only alternative we have, the only weapon available."[57]

Carlos Flores, the director of Chile's film school, believes that digital technology will make room for new forms of narrative film that are closer to daily life and advertising productions, likely to encourage major changes in the industry, to attract a new generation of young filmmakers who are a long way from the Hollywood model, and to provide a quick resolution to current distribution problems.

The economic crisis in Argentina, a country with a strong film tradition, may delay the deployment of digital technology, but there will be a lot of interest in it, particularly given that the country's national institute of film and audiovisual arts, the Instituto Nacional de Cine y Artes Audiovisuales, or INCAA, intends to establish quotas to protect national film production against a Hollywood invasion.

India is the largest film producer in the world, creating some 1,000 films per year, and is a significant potential market for digital film. Bollywood (the Hollywood of Bombay, now Mumbai) is well known, but the Indian film industry is also active in other cities, in particular in Madras, Hyderabad, and Bangalore. An estimated 20 million people go to the movies every day in India, and some 3 billion go annually, for a population of 1 billion! Hollywood has made very few inroads into India, though some of the majors (Twentieth Century Fox and Warner Bros) opened offices there a few years ago. Contrary to established thought, India exports films, particularly to places with Indian immigrant communities, such as Great Britain, Western Africa, and the United States. But Indian culture appears to have protected the country from an invasion of American films, which garner modest box-office receipts in a few multiplexes in large cities.

At the end of 2004, India, which has 12,000 theatres equipped with 35 mm technology, already had several hundred digital theatres, and the industry has announced that by 2005 there will be 1,600. Of course India's size, density, difficulty of getting around—particularly during monsoon season—hot, humid climate, and limited financial resources are not favourable to the high cost of traditional film reels. So digital media and satellite transmission will do well in the country, which also has Bangalore, a veritable Silicon Valley of IT professionals who can find quick, effective solutions for servers and digital compression, transmission, management, and security software. Subhash Ghai, president of Mukta Arts, elaborates, "With the rising costs of production work in the traditional style of film making, the digital cinema technology has come as a boon. For the producers, it is also one of the most innovative and modern trends to curb piracy."[58] Given the size of the country, films on digital media could circulate for months, reaching far-flung villages, affordably and with no deterioration in master quality, even several years after a film is released in Mumbai or New Delhi, something which is currently impossible. The digital film business model is a shoo-in in India more than anywhere else, and promises formerly unimaginable profits.

The year 2004 marked a first: the satellite distribution of the film *Bardashdt*, from servers in Mumbai and Noida to 25 theatres in the states of Delhi, Uttar Pradesh, Punjab, and Haryana. Dev Digital Cinema, the company that undertook this initiative, is partner to Ginni Arts, Bobby Arts, and Adlabs, owned by Shringar Films, India's largest film distributor. Digital technology should thus make it possible to reach new audiences in India, who at the moment are poorly served or not served at all by distributors, and should also make it possible to save on production and distribution, potentially generating a boom in the film industry in a country that is poorly covered by television networks and that is, as a result, more receptive to film. Rajeev Gupta, owner of Delhi-based Wave Cineplexes, part of the Ginni Arts group, has also been seduced by the potential savings from digital technology: "Instead of spending.Rs 50,000 or Rs 60,000 per print, the costs will work out to Rs 5,000 to Rs 7,000 per theatre."[59] The president of Adlabs Films, Manmohan Shetty, is considering installing digital technology in up to 400 theatres in India, and Mukta Arts and Adlabs Films are planning to equip all of India very soon.

Bollywood is going to go digital, and India is currently the largest market that will adopt end-to-end digital film and support the development of reasonably priced satellite distribution technologies or 1K or 2K DVD distribution, orders from Hollywood notwithstanding.

Besides, India has many official languages, and digital technology makes dubbing better and more affordable. Several soundtracks can coexist on the same hard drive, allowing for broader circulation than with 35 mm reels and eliminating the considerable expense of prints. At the end of 2003, Bollywood even entered into negotiations with the American company Kazaa for paid worldwide distribution of films via the internet. It's another way of exporting its productions to the 20 million expat Indians in the world, for whom the appeal of direct contact with their culture could induce them to compromise on the quality and format of viewing, making a computer screen acceptable.

China already had some 300 digital theatres in 2004. And the China Film Group Corporation, the largest importer and distributor of films in China, has announced its intention to move progressively toward digital distribution and to equip

2,500 theatres digitally in the next five years. The company, which is a government corporation, has already signed an agreement with Alpha Spacecom, the stated goal of which is to save on the cost of film reels, but the objective may also be to encourage more independent films, Chinese films in particular, and to serve more remote areas. In 2004, the company Christie had already equipped more than 50 Chinese theatres with digital projectors. China is the largest market in the world, and it is preparing to go digital, for the same reasons as India and Latin America, regardless of what Hollywood says; the country is not going to submit to the DC28's ridiculous standards. China will carry its weight ...

The government of Singapore, which has a special relationship with Hollywood, nonetheless decided in 2003 to implement 21 2K digital theatres, including in the new Eng Wah multiplex. According to Thomas Lim, Singapore's director of games and entertainment, "The world's first digital multiplex by Eng Wah is testimony of Singapore's overall commitment to develop the local digital cinema industry. Singapore is now a step closer in our quest to be a leading global Digital Exchange where not just capital, people and ideas but also digital assets come together."[60] This initiative will create a local industry of digital services that could generate 5,000 new jobs within three years, according to the Infocomm Development Authority. The government's objective is to create a digital film technology centre of expertise to serve all of Southwest Asia.

In Canada, a bit closer to the U.S., the country's 4,000 movie theatres are in a sense integrated into the American market. To combat this situation, the NFB has opted for digital cinema and at the end of 2003 decided to promote a national alternative network, at the initiative of its president, Jacques Bensimon, who is also Government Film Commissioner. The English Canadian identity is obviously very fragile, given the common language and the free trade agreement with the powerful U.S.; it is definitely more vulnerable than the identity of Quebecers, a minority that protects its linguistic identity and has an age-old tradition of resistance. The NFB wants to combat the existing means of distribution that promotes uniform cultural expression, to increase access in Canada to Canadian products like documentaries and auteur films. The Canadian government has set the objective to have Canadian films account for 5% of box-office revenue in 2006. Jacques Bensimon is convinced that documentaries can contribute to achieving this objective and that digital distribution is the way to get there.

Laurie Jones, director of communications and outreach development at the NFB, explains, "This new network will rely on digital technology, because digital makes it possible to keep the cost of prints low and to substantially reduce the costs of production, distribution, and projection, even in outlying regions and the North. For example, digital technology and satellite will make it possible to screen an independent film nationally. Satellite also makes it possible to organize debates with filmmakers simultaneously in all theatres."[61]

The Toronto International Film Festival is interesting in this respect, because it has expanded its programming beyond its walls. The Film Circuit presents new films in independent theatres and now reaches more than 300,000 new spectators through some 2,000 screenings in more than 100 communities in Canada. According to Jacques Bensimon, the NFB also hopes to find new audiences, in university theatres, municipal libraries, museums, and community centres. And he insists that this is a return to the original mandate of the NFB as it was created by John Grierson, who in the 1950s emphasized the importance of the NFB putting into place its own alternative distribution network. Digital technology is facilitating a return to the social mandate of film, to its ability to contribute to debate, moving well beyond the Hollywood reduction that has turned the art form into a mere entertainment industry. It is therefore a question of positioning Canada on the world chessboard of digital film, according to a schedule started in 2004.

It is ironic that at the very same moment, the director of Telefilm Canada was negotiating the exact opposite with the American Creative Art Agency (which has among its ranks the oh-so-Hollywood Steven Spielberg, Tom Cruise, and Julia Roberts) to co-produce Canadian films with American partners to, according to media reports, ensure that they are distributed in the United States and perhaps even in large international circuits. This once again imposes the logic of Hollywood imperialism, which has infiltrated even the vision of those in the government whose responsibility it is to defend and promote film production in their own country. Telefilm Canada, unlike the NFB, arranged things thusly, in spite of the outraged protests of Canadian professionals and producers who are part of the Alliance of Canadian Cinema, Television and Radio Artists (ACTRA), a de facto supporter of American uniformity, if indeed the project goes ahead.

Among private initiatives in Quebec, obviously Daniel Langlois's efforts merit mention as they are intended to set up a network of independent digital theatres in other countries as well: Europe, India, China, and even in the U.S.! He raised the issue in 2004 at the fifth anniversary of Ex-Centris: "Satellite makes it possible to reach any theatre, anywhere in the world. We have approached countries in Asia. In India, China, and Indonesia, people in film want a technology that works, and they are prepared to deploy it quickly."[62]

The Rise of Anti-Americanism and Digital Anti-globalization

The movement is becoming widespread. In Africa too, the future of film lies in digital technology and satellite distribution, as it does in Indonesia, the Philippines, and in the vast territories of Central Europe. Digital technology will be the key to inexpensive national film production and will let large numbers of people who are currently deprived of film gain access to it. All countries have the right to their own film culture, and only digital technology will take us in that direction. That's one good thing about the globalization of digital technology.

Circumstances are now favourable: there is the rise of digital technology in film combined with the loss of credibility of American culture throughout the world. A market study conducted by NOP World in 2004 of 300,000 consumers in 30 countries between 13 and 65 years of age, at a rate of 10,000 people in each country, showed the rising planet-wide disrepute of the U.S. and its culture: the American way of life, a mythical symbol of Hollywood film, is losing its hold and is increasingly coming under attack. Is this really the case? NOP World is the New York arm of the British company United Business Media, which can hardly be accused of anti-Americanism.

———

NOTES

46. European Commission, "Conclusions of the Seminar on the Monitoring of the Cinema Communication on the Future of the Film and Audiovisual Industry: Aspects Relating to Heritage Preservation, Digital Cinema, Cinematrographic Education and the Rating of Films," Seville, May 7, 2002, 7–8.

47. European Space Agency, "ESA Contributes to Development of Digital and Electronic Cinema in Europe," news release, August 28, 2003, http://www.esa.int/esaCP/Pr_52_2003_p_EN.html

48. Richard Morris speaking at National Film Board of Canada, e-cinema conference, http://www.nfb.ca/launchers/?id=53.

49. Ibid.

50. Kees Ryninks speaking at National Film Board of Canada, e-cinema conference, http://www.nfb.ca/launchers/?id=53.

51. Perreault, "Un exemple européen: Docuzone."

52. Patrick Caradec "Digital Beach fait la part belle au numerique," le film français.com, May 23, 2002, http://www.lefilmfrancais.com/cannes2002/pages/230502.htm

53. Andrew Downie, "Brazil Takes Lead Role in Move to All-digital Cinema," *The Christian Science Monitor*, February 5, 2004, http://www.csmonitor.com/2004/0205/p07s01-woam.html

54. Omar Gonzalez, President, ICAIC, in discussion with the author, 2004.

55. Juan Carlos Tamayo, "¿Mito, Fantasía, Pobreza o Realidad?" *Utopia Webmagazine USFQ*, 2004.

· 56. "Cine digital llegó para quedarse," *Chile.com*, http://www.chile.com/tpl/articulo/detalle/masnotas.tpl?cod_articulo=1581

57. Ibid.

58. B. B. Oberoi, "Digital Films Click with Cinegoers," *The Tribune*, January 12, 2004, http://www.tribuneindia.com/2004/20040112/login/main4.htm

59. Aparna Kalra, "E-cinema: Coming Soon to a Theatre Near You," *Times News Network*, March 23, 2004.

60. Government of Singapore, "Singapore Announces The World's First Full Digital Multiplex," news release, March 22, 2004.

61. Laurie Jones, Director of Communications and Outreach Development, National Film Board of Canada, in discussion with the author.

62. Stéphane Baillargeon, "Cinq ans et toutes ses dents," *Le Devoir*, May 1, 2004.

WOODY ALLEN VS. HOLLOW WOOD

Independent film can be revived—in a number of countries it already has been. In Quebec, for example, according to Quebec's official statistics body, the Institut de la statistique, audiences for Quebec movies grew from 6.1% in 2001, to 8.8% in 2002, to 13% in 2003, although attendance for Hollywood films maintained an average of at least 78%. So there is already hope, although digital film has not yet turned the stats on their heads.

In the U.S., Woody Allen is the symbol of independent film, a unique anti-star who has rejected the Hollywood studio system. For this we honour him, in the name of the auteur film and the independent film of which the Americans have deprived themselves and other parts of the world.

By delivering us from Hollywood's hegemony, digital technology is going to help us rediscover repertory film. For years movie lovers have had to settle for poor quality VHS cassettes to see the great films in the history of cinema, which theatres no longer screen, either because of block booking, or because the 35 mm reels are no longer available for the independent theatre owners who want to screen one from time to time. Unless you live near a cinematheque. Cinematheques generally only have a limited selection of old films that they protect because they don't have the budget for new prints, you simply can't see many of these classic films. And they are not all available on VHS or DVD, not by a long shot.

Commercial theatres generally show films that have just been released and only for the duration of their immediate success, which is sometimes quite ephemeral. Of course, the majors have a treasure trove of still-famous old films, but they are no longer shown. And as we have seen, they plan to use them to generate revenue by making them available on the internet, offering affordable downloads, but also mediocre viewing conditions. It will be like looking at a masterpiece reproduced on a stamp.

But it's digital distribution that will allow theatre owners to screen old repertory films alongside new films, in optimal conditions on a large screen. There is much at stake with digital distribution, if only for the precious gift of letting us see repertory films as they were meant to be seen, on a big screen. As DigiScreen's Pierre Latour points out, how many years has it been since we were able to see Hal Ashby's masterpiece *Harold and Maud* and so many other great films? Plus, with digital technology we would be able to watch them without seeing evidence of the ravages of time, the scratches and tears on old reels; digital technology will restore films to the quality of the original master print and even make it possible to restore the master from damaged film, as was done with the Georges Méliès films that could be found.

Digital technology could also help bring documentary and activist film back, which had been feared an endangered genre. But Michael Moore's *Bowling for Columbine* proved that this wasn't the case. When he made *Fahrenheit 9/11*, Disney-owned Miramax refused to distribute it for fear of displeasing the Republican Party. But Lions Gate Films snapped it up, and the movie earned a record-breaking $21.8 million in box-office receipts in its first week, rather than the forecast total of $10 million for its entire run. It could earn $200 million or more worldwide. It turned out that distributors were eventually fighting over it because of the topicality of the anti-Bush controversy and the Golden Palm it received at the Cannes Festival, so that in a few hours the number of U.S. theatres showing it jumped from a hundred to close to a thousand. It beat documentary sales records in every country, from Great Britain to Cuba, the latter of which showed a pirated, subtitled version in 120 theatres and on television four weeks after the movie's release in the United States, with a glee we can only imagine!

Remarkably, that year the Cannes Festival actually selected *two* activist documentaries for its official competition, the other being Jonathan Nossiter's *Mondovino*, which criticizes the role of multinationals in the fine wine market.

Since its beginnings the National Film Board of Canada has promoted the social documentary and is doing so now more than ever with retrospectives and new titles on television, in theatres, and through its online cinematheque. In Quebec with its particularly young audiences, demand for documentary is increasing. In 2004, the NFB started showing an interesting selection of six documentaries as part of Québécois tout court. Ex-Centris now shows more political, anti-globalization, and environmental documentaries, movies that are well attended, such as Richard Desjardins and Robert Monderie's *Forest Alert*, which speaks out against clear cutting, Hugo Latulippe's *Bacon*, which takes a position against the pollution caused by large hog houses; and *The Corporation*, by Canadians Mark Achbar, Jennifer Abbot, and Joel Bakan, a low-budget film ($1.1 million) that has done very well internationally, including in the U.S., which shows the cynicism of multinationals. Monique Simard, president of the Quebec documentary producer Productions Virage, points out, "For the past seven years, the number of socio-political documentaries has increased by 500% in the industrialized world. Hard-hitting leftie projects are in. They're what's selling and what broadcasters are asking for." She adds, "Since the attacks on the World Trade Center and the war in Iraq, people have been worried about where the world is heading, and they need to understand it in order to combat the feeling of powerlessness. There is a very strong anti-American undercurrent."[63] Irène Bignardi of the Locarno Film Festival points to the trend as well, saying that documentaries can help decipher the unstable world we live in. And in 2004, one of the Quebec government arts bodies, the Société de développement des entreprises culturelles du Québec (SODEC), showed support for this revival of documentary by financing 16 documentaries, several of them for commercial theatres.

In Europe, DocuZone is counting on a new interest in documentary. Docspace is its partner in Great Britain, and the European Digital Film Festival will present documentaries in eight European countries simultaneously.

The rise of digital technology is also a return to independent film. Lots of movies that can't be made today, due to inflated production budgets resulting from Hollywood competition and due to the cost of producing films in 35 mm, will get made thanks to the much more modest investment required for digital shoots. Every day, gradually, major filmmakers like Lars von Trier are setting the example. The more favourable conditions are going to create a new generation of social and political documentaries, as well as auteur films, which, rather than remaining orphans, could be distributed in the independent theatre networks that will be formed, thanks to digital technology.

Much has been said about the small budget for Michael Moore's *Fahrenheit 9/11*. Jonathan Caouette's *Tarnation*, and *Troy*, were also made with a small budget. On all sides, independent film is going through a rebirth, thanks to the advantages of digital technology. But we still need a revival of independent theatres to screen these independent films, like Quebecer Robert Lepage's *Far Side of the Moon*.

Digital technology even makes non-budget film a possibility, an authentic, high-quality, low-budget genre that has appeared in emerging countries. The Cuban filmmaker Humberto Solas talks about the financial and cultural problems these countries face: "If you make a film with contributions from two other countries, then you're obliged to pass through a process of domestication. You have to please different cultures. Generally speaking, we don't co-produce films among ourselves—there aren't any Cuba-Brazil, Cuba-Mexico, or Cuba-Argentine films. It's the same for them as it is for us; there are more possibilities of dialogue, common discourse. But when you make a film with Holland, Germany or France, you can be sure that there will be no cultural confrontation; that's not what it's about. The supposition is that a co-production will create a common discourse—you would undoubtedly be obliged to take into consideration aspects that are not relevant to one's idiosyncrasies or cultural and national identity."[64] For him, making films with a limited budget is important because these types of films make it possible to express the nuances of one's own culture, which is preferable to a carefully measured blend of cultures or to uniformity. "Less compromise means more freedom," he says.[65]

Film has no greater calling to multiculturalism than other cultural creations. Made-in-Hollywood universalism, as Humberto Solas calls it, is a globalizing cinema of compromise that tries to merge different cultural traits and to find the common denominator that will make it palatable everywhere on the planet. But according to Solas, to create local, national, identity-based film, with an intensity of authentic expression, working with a small budget is better. And that's precisely what digital technology permits, offering emerging countries a historic chance to develop a national cinema. And distribution via digital film networks will take these films out of their ghetto.

Besides, developed countries are experiencing a backlash in the form of an anti-Hollywood sentiment and are launching initiatives to provide poor countries with greater access to cinema. In Africa, France's Centre national de la cinématographie, the European Development Fund, the Agence intergouvernementale de la Francophonie, UNICEF, and many other European and African partners (Benin, Niger, Mali) have taken the initiative to create the Cinéma numérique ambulant (CNA), a sort of mobile movie unit that organizes public screenings of African films in villages. These productions deal with all sorts of current events through cartoons, shorts, and long features, all of them African, which without this initiative to provide travelling digital projection equipment would not be able to find a distribution network. The mandate of the organization underlines this: "Travelling cinema has already proven itself, in Africa and elsewhere. Nevertheless, the shortage of theatres is so striking in Africa that the idea of travelling cinema is essential, even as a resolutely modern concept. In new technology there are critical responses to the problem of a lack of distribution infrastructure in Africa."[66]

The CNA has therefore developed mobile projection units: "The lightweight character of digital technology makes all dreams possible. The CNA takes advantage of the technological advances of digital technology and DVD to screen movies in ideal technical conditions in outlying or isolated villages that are often off the beaten path of the main routes of communication."[67] The lightweight kit consists of a video projector, two DVD and VHS players, a generator, a 4x3-metre screen, a sound system, a vehicle, three local presenters trained and paid by the CNA, and a driver. CNA teams visit each village ten times, around once every two weeks, each time with different programming. The investment is minimal compared to the cost of setting up a traditional movie theatre. And admission is free in exchange for services provided by the village to prepare the site, store the equipment, and so on. The experiment started in Benin in 2001. At the end of 2003, it had already drawn some 500,000 spectators.

In Latin America, Swiss filmmaker Stefan Kaspar has founded another interesting initiative—the Association Grupo Cine Latino: "Digital technology offers a potential, a force of decentralization and democratization to increase access to the audiovisual arts. It can even be a driver of development to provide greater visibility to Latin American culture."[68] And he points out that in emerging countries, digital technology reduces the costs of production and distribution by 75% or more. In fact, like elsewhere, globalization has encouraged concentration in ownership of theatres in developing countries, following the lead of Hollywood distribution networks, and as a result theatres in poor neighbourhoods and small towns have disappeared. This trend has also excluded poorer audiences, due to the high price of admission. "Digital technology will open a new chapter," Kaspar adds. "Digital cinema is going to be a revolution, as if the film industry were to start from scratch under new conditions. And the most important thing is that digital technology will make it possible to show films that represent the richness and diversity of authentic local cinema."[69] Having larger national audiences who can reappropriate their own film culture will result in new sources of financing for national filmmakers.

In Canada in 2004, in partnership with aboriginal institutions, the NFB set up a training and travelling cinema project to help break the social isolation of First Nations peoples. The project involves a truck and trailer, the Wapikoni—named in memory of a young aboriginal leader who helped improve the lot of his Attikamek community—which has a mini production studio and digital projection equipment and travels across the territory of the Attikamek and Algonquin reserves. Young aboriginals can use the equipment to produce short features on their issues, which are shown on websites and as part of events such as the First Peoples' Festival. Headed by Manon Barbeau, a filmmaker who is involved in youth issues (*L'armée de l'ombre*, 2000), this project is as much about society as it is about cinema: "If young aboriginal people reconnect with their roots and their history and at the same time open up to the world, they will create a connection with us that will offer something extremely precious."[70] This sort of initiative is in line with the original social mandate of the NFB, NFB president Jacques Bensimon points out.

Digital technology has also helped increase the number of festivals. Of course, they are virtually all alternative festivals by Hollywood standards, because they show mainly non-Hollywood films. The director of the Copenhagen International Film Festival, Janne Viese, said in 2004, "We want to create an ode above all to European film. Not all European films are good, but there are plenty that are remarkable, that deserve to be brought out of the shadows and take their place in distributors' catalogues, who for the most part swear by Hollywood."[71] There are hundreds of festivals that in one way or another celebrate different types of film and that have been a source of hope to many independent filmmakers over the years, in the face of the unyielding law of the empire. Started by Claude Chamberlan and Dimitri Epides in 1971, the Festival du nouveau cinéma is well known in Quebec, but there is a whole network of other film festivals around the world.

Even Hollywood star Robert Redford showed his support for independent film by launching the Sundance Institute Festival. At the premiere of *The Clearing*, he said, "Of course it's becoming harder and harder to unearth interesting projects in Hollywood. Everything is oriented toward the young audiences that fill up multiplexes."[72]

In a very different context, Cuban filmmaker Humberto Solas also takes a position: "In the midst of Cuban cinema's economic crisis, due to something we all know about, I was able to make a film that would have been impossible if I'd used 35-mm, so I made it in digital film. I'm talking about *Miel para Oshún* (*Honey for Oshún*). That whole experience led me to conclude that I had to dig a trench in Cuba, the ideal country to do so, where creators—not just Cuban, but from all over the world—would be able to have the chance to attend a festival where, if their work does well, it means something concrete to them: the possibility of continuing their careers."[73] As a result, he launched the Non-Budget Film Festival. And in Montreal, Claude Chamberlan created the "No-Budget Film Festival"—the Festival du film fauché—exclusively for mini-budget productions. Cinema is stepping down from its chauffeur-driven stretch limo to become more democratic. It's going to become about the people again.

Documentary festivals are springing up everywhere, for example, the Sheffield Touring International Documentary Film Festival in Great Britain, the Montreal International Documentary Film Festival, Hot Docs in Toronto, the Festival de Noyon in Switzerland, Marseille's Sunny Side of the Doc, Lyon's Festival international cinéma nouvelle generation (which shows films in different locations, including feature films and guerrilla movies shot digitally), the Festival international du film francophone de Namur in Belgium, the Fespaco du Burkina Faso, which is crucial to African film, and so many others, all of which have been successful and are drawing larger audiences.

For some, digital technology offers not only the possibility of distribution independent of Hollywood, but also of equitable distribution, because it can reach people in rural and outlying areas. This is one of the NFB's mandates in Canada. In Great Britain, Paul Kafno, managing director of HD Thames, launched Cinenet, a network of electronic theatres that has spread throughout Europe, and films live shows in Germany, France, Belgium, and Spain. In France, the 1994 implementation of a high-resolution video transmission network, the VTHR, is meant to make up for the absence of theatres in rural areas and offers quality retransmissions in areas outside of major cities. It has 300 fully equipped theatres, many of them located in town halls or municipal buildings. It even allowed fans to watch soccer's World Cup! And Omar Gonzalez, the president of the ICAIC, has also chosen this approach; the Cuban government can offer the entire population not only educational and public health services, but also electronic access to film and rebroadcasts of major cultural events through the internet network that connects cities and small towns.

Of course we must not forget the growing number of alternative sites that reach new audiences: cafés like the Café Méliès, Café Lumière, Café DVD, Café Écran Noir, and Cinéma Café; events like outdoor film screenings through Nuits blanches du cinéma, Magnifico, and film events for children. These phenomena hearken back to small projection rooms at fairs in the early days of cinema, which people like Georges Méliès supplied with films. This may be yet one more sign of a rebirth of cinema.

This rebirth obviously assumes that new business models are adopted for independent film. According to Richard Morris, formerly of the UK Film Council, "A lot of cinemas are actually not full. Exhibitors want to fill their seats. A lot of the exhibitors in the U.K. are happy to say, 'Okay, let's stick in a mid-range digital system to handle specialized film in one of our screens. Perfect. Or two or our screens. Let's try it.' But we need to do that now, while that window of opportunity exists ... Your average movie theatre is totally empty; in the UK we have a lot of wasted time in these venues. Surely that's not a great business model. Surely we can be doing more. So that's ultimately what this game is about, especially from an exhibitor's point of view."[74]

Digital management of royalties, which will be needed to ensure the sustainability of new business models, does not pose a challenge. Because digital media, servers, and even projectors offer the ability to encrypt films to avoid pirating and to count the number of screenings, a figure which can automatically be sent via the internet to the distributor. It will be hard to get around the system, which is currently vulnerable because of videocassettes, DVDs, and internet downloads: these practices will soon be a thing of the past.

Cinema is also a social ritual that takes place in front of a screen. Popcorn is clearly part of that ritual: in fact concession sales keep some theatres from bankruptcy. But the new upsurge in movie audiences confirms what defines film, perhaps above all else: the size of the screen and the ritual of sharing a powerful cultural experience.

Of course, some people, major filmmakers among them, are asking whether cinema is going to become tedious to the point of theatres closing, replaced by increasingly sophisticated home theatre equipment or more modestly by DVD players and home TV screens. While there is a trend toward home theatres among the very rich who outfit their basements, movie lovers who have no other way to see film classics, and young people who trade DVDs and watch them in the basements of their parents' homes, in my view movie theatres are no more likely to disappear than are paper copies of books; on the contrary, because the film industry, like the publishing industry, offers products for social use—rituals—that home screens can in no way replace, be they large, in high definition, interactive, in colour and stereo sound, and offering the comfort of home viewing, books and theatres will instead multiply in the future. They will proliferate not only in emerging countries where ordinary people do not have the means to set up home theatres, but also in rich countries, once digital technology makes it possible for theatres to show quality, repertory, and new, independent films; as Hollywood films go from bad to worse, audiences are more reluctant to spend their money and their Saturday night going to the cinema to take in a turkey. The reduced attendance for art and experimental theatres in 2006 in Canada, on the heels of a strong increase in previous years, cannot be attributed solely to the success of DVD, but is rather the result of the cycles and volatility of cultural habits. Movie attendance also depends a great deal on the size of promotional budgets, and the crisis in Hollywood, which has become increasingly evident in 2006, has no doubt had a temporary negative effect on the behaviour of movie audiences.

But let's assume that I'm wrong and that movie theatres disappear because of DVD. DVD will still mark the end of the 35 mm reel and the Hollywood empire, resulting in a fragmentation of the movie market and major flexibility in new social uses and movie audiences. The film industry would look more like the music or publishing industries, and Hollywood would not be able to stop the proliferation of local publishing and independent houses. Profits would be reduced, even if the DVD market were to become very lucrative, and would no longer allow for the massive advertising campaigns for blockbusters, to which Hollywood owes a large part of its past success, along with its impending financial ruin.

As long as there is a screen and a projector, audiences will gather. Let the ritual begin ... One of the strangest of these rituals is cineoke, where amateurs act out cult scenes in front of screens where the movie is projected, drawing on the models of karaoke and theatre improvisation, like Quebec's national improvisation league—the Ligue nationale d'improvisation. Under the leadership of Claude Chamberlan, New York, Paris, and now Montreal participate in this gregarious, joyful cinematographic dance.

There has also been a sudden upsurge in Kino groups, which started in Quebec in 1999 and are now active in several countries under the name Planet Kino. Amateur filmmakers, called kinoites, produce short features with a digital camera and then share them with each other at screenings. The three principles are: Do well with nothing. Do better with little. Do it right now. No doubt future filmmakers will rise from their ranks. There are also long Kinos, evenings devoted to screening short features followed by debates with the filmmakers, which the Europeans hold in their DocuZone theatres. Discussions follow the themes of films and can include the ecology, politics, health issues, spirituality, psychology, relationships, and more. A far cry from the Hollywood machine, there is a resurgent vitality among movie lovers that bodes well for the future of film.

The multimedia aspect of digital technologies may also contribute substantially to this style of interactive film, which clearly interests audiences.

Digital technology is prompting a return to cultural diversity. According to the figures available, there are between 160,000 and 200,000 theatres worldwide. Imagine the moment, which is imminent, when they are all equipped with digital equipment! Their numbers will increase to around 250,000 or 300,000! They won't all be equipped for high-definition digital projection, and maybe 50,000 will be equipped for lower-definition e-cinema, or electronic cinema, but they will still satisfy new audiences by offering the same variety of programming as HD theatres.

Even cinematheques tend to jealously guard their 35 mm reels in their vaults, only screening digital copies. In fact, Hollywood's obstruction of digital distribution is encouraging the growth of independent theatre networks equipped more modestly but no less effectively, stealing Hollywood's market share, one that it will never be able to recoup or control.

But what do the filmmakers themselves think? Some don't want to weigh in given that Hollywood is still the market leader. Some take reactionary or nostalgic positions, others don't ask the question, and yet others are already campaigning for digital technology. Attitudes vary when it comes to these questions.

"I am a Luddite," Steven Spielberg has said (a term coined for John Ludd, the Brit who, at the end of the 19th century, launched campaigns to destroy machines, which were seen as provoking endemic unemployment), clearly signalling his mistrust of digital distribution. According to Spielberg, even if ten years from now many theatres are equipped with digital technology, there will still be projection rooms with 35 mm to cater to filmmakers like him who like the look of movies on film.[75] And he doesn't believe any more than I do in watching films on computer screens.

Spielberg, who uses naturalism as masterfully as special effects in his films, may be right in his view that digital technology is not as big a change as the arrival of sound or colour in film, at least from the point of view of production. But unlike his friend George Lucas, what he has not completely understood is that the digital revolution also involves distribution. This is undoubtedly because distribution is not a problem for him: he is a privileged Hollywood filmmaker, and he has no reason to complain about the power of the cartel that distributes his films! Of course, his films often express a mistrust of technology and science, in the name of traditional humanism.

But George Lucas, who is as much a Hollywood icon as Spielberg, has a much more radical view. He believes in digital film from A to Z, for distribution as well as for production, perhaps because he is immersed in the world of science fiction. And he demonstrated a willingness to go digital beginning in 2002, with *Star Wars, Episode 2: Attack of the Clones.* Steven Spielberg didn't miss the opportunity to comment reservedly on the call from George Lucas for an increase in the number of theatres equipped for digital projection: "I would do anything for my friend George Lucas, including compromising my own belief system. But I think practically speaking, there aren't going to be enough theaters even in 2005 to exhibit digital film to make it worth my while to commit digitally to Indy 4 at this time. If there were 2,000 screens with digital projectors I might seriously consider it for George and his vision of the future. But it looks like there's no chance that the theaters will put it in the next three years, so I'll be happily shooting Indy 4 on film."[76]

Are the growing numbers of filmmakers who opt for digital technology simply ahead of their time?

In 1999, Canadian David Cronenberg, commenting on his film *eXistenZ* to critic Andy Spletzer, said, "We're all aware that we're in a transitional medium right now, and the transition is to digital. My next movie I might be shooting direct to hard drive. I'm not interested in being the first, because I don't care about that. I'd rather do it when it's mature and stable. George Lucas is on a different mind-set and all of that, but in fact, we all know it's going to happen. There's no question about it."[77]

Many filmmakers have used digital technology, some occasionally and some systematically: names that count like Lars von Trier, Claude Miller, Luc Besson, and Atom Egoyan.

The filmmaking giant, Ingmar Bergman, in launching his made-for-TV-movie *Saraband* at the World Film Festival in Montreal in 2004, said that he refused to have his film blown up to 35 mm and insisted that it be shown in theatres equipped with digital technology. In 2004, at the Festival du nouveau cinéma, British filmmaker Peter Greenaway and producer Kees Kasander premiered the complete *Tulse Luper Suitcases*, a multimedia work including a film shot and distributed in high definition, a website, and an interactive game.

Why are so many others still resisting the move to digital technology, not only for production, but also for projection? George Lucas answers the question, in a fascinating interview with Michael Goldman, "It's true that HD has certain unique characteristics that a lot of people complain about. But film has them too—it's always had them, and they aren't necessarily that flattering to look at. It's just that film's flaws are built into the system—everyone has been using it for so long that no one recognizes the flaws anymore. No one wants to talk about them. People just maneuver around them silently, pretending they are not there, like big elephants that sit around the room. They pretend not to see the film elephant, but they point out the digital elephant ... So why stick with a medium that is limited as a technology, developed in the 19th century?" He adds, "[There are people in this industry who] are still fighting it tooth and nail. They are also doing everything they can to stall digital projection in theaters, even though those systems are obviously higher quality ... People say that digital projection in theaters is not quite 'there' yet, whatever that means. But they must not have ever seen a release print in its fourth or fifth week in a typical theater."[78]

63. Odile Tremblay, "Cinéma documentaire: le retour," *Le Devoir*, July 3, 2004.

64. Mireya Castaneda, "Non-budget film festival: a great endeavour," CubaNow.net, http://www.cubanow.cult.cu/global/loader.php?secc=8&cont=films/num10/1.htm

65. Ibid.

66. Cinemasfrancophones.org, "Associations professionnelles, http://www.cinemasfrancophones.org/fiches/paysFrance/carnets/Associations_pro fessionnelles/

67. CNA, "Cinéma Numérique Ambulant," http://www.c-n-a.org/cna.html

68. Alberto Dufey, "Las nuevas tecnologías para desarrollar el cine," *Swissinfo*, December 3, 2003, http://www2.swissinfo.org/ses/swissinfo.html?siteSect=2105&sid=4472121&cKey=1070436224000

69. Ibid.

70. Jean-Guillaume Dumont, "Rompre l'isolement par la creation," *Le Devoir*, June 12, 2004.

71. Slim Allagui, "Copenhague, vitrine du cinema européen," *Le Devoir*, August 18, 2004, B7.

72. Marc-André Lussier, "The Clearing: Redford le magnifique," *La Presse*, "Cinema," July 3, 2004, 3.

73. Mireya Castaneda, "Non-budget Film Festival: A Great Endeavour," CubaNow.net, http://www.cubanow.net/global/loader.php?secc=8&cont=films/num10/1.htm

74. Richard Morris, e-cinema conference.

75. "A Movie-making Luddite," *The Economist*, December 19, 2002.

76. *Empire Magazine*, January 2003.

77. Andy Spletzer, "New Sexual Organs: An Interview with David Cronenberg," *The Stranger*, April 29–May 5, 1999, http://www.thestranger.com/seattle/Content?oid=897

78. Goldman, "The Luca POV."

The Last Hollywood Picture Show

Hollywood has run out of imagination. Profits—an obsession on the scale of Hollywood budgets and the resultant ever-increasing risks that the empire imposes on itself—are foremost in the minds of producers, who have abandoned the art of film. Dismally failed remakes and other blockbusters—including the frightful *Da Vinci Code, Superman Returns, King Kong,* and the *X-Men* sequels, *X2* and *X-Men: The Last Stand,* will not only destroy Hollywood, but will also discourage the public from going to the movies. Of course, Hollywood makes attempts to redeem itself through its psuedo-indies—the independents that they control—producing better films for less money without losing face. But it is unlikely that the system gives independent filmmakers enough creative freedom to restore the artistic quality of American cinema and to fill up the theatres in its worldwide network. Hollywood can only maintain its empire through high-quality blockbuster successes with their massive budgets. The system is simply untenable, and as of 2006, there is no longer any doubt that Hollywood has reached its limits and is starting to fall. With the advent of digital distribution, the film industry will fragment, diversify, and take root again in national cultures, which will enjoy new life and visibility. Logic is not on Hollywood's side. I wrote the French version of this book in 2004, and in 2006, my predictions are already being borne out.

Will we regret the decline of an empire that has been so merciless in imposing its law? Few tears will be shed for the big seven. There will be no requiem, because Hollywood has helped destroy independent, auteur, and national film.

Would you like to see a Hollywood film? Or a Hollywood film? That's how Hollywood works.

The government of Singapore, for example, has understood that the dynamic of digital film is sustained by the exponential development of new technologies in general, and will contribute in turn to their development, putting one more nail in the coffin of 35 mm. It's only Hollywood that refuses to understand. Suppliers of film equipment, even the most traditional like Kodak, are turning toward digital, as was evident at NAB 2004 in Las Vegas, the most important annual event for the industry, which that particular year was festooned with the banner *Go beyond!*

This critical turn of the tide could be sudden and quickly submerge the Hollywood cartel, a behemoth that moves much slower than independent production and distribution networks. Schooners can change course in time to avoid an iceberg looming suddenly. But the *Titanic*, in spite of the pride and arrogance that surrounded it, in spite of its luxury and fame, sank. The perfect Hollywood film that could spawn a sequel—*Titanic 2*—one that Hollywood hasn't thought of yet, but which could be the film of its ruin.

Of course, as Claude Chamberlan, director of Montreal's Festival du nouveau cinéma points out, Hollywood's craftspeople devote their lives to film. So we will be sorry to see them lose jobs, but this regret will be tempered by seeing so many other jobs created around the world. And initially, a crisis in Hollywood will lead to the loss of jobs in Canada, but only briefly.

In the name of cultural diversity, freedom of expression, and creativity in film, which will no longer be subject to the single-minded logic of maximum profit and American-style globalization, we will rejoice in the imminent end of this hegemony. We will soon be able to enjoy a good old Hollywood film in a repertory theatre in a small town off the beaten path, in high-definition digital.

Ironically, right when Hollywood is sure that it has succeeded in imposing its movies worldwide, the unstoppable wave of the digital revolution is rising up and reaching the Hollywood Hills. The famous Hollywood sign is already pixelizing. *The day after tomorrow* has begun, and the hurricane will submerge the sacred hills, just as this blockbuster predicted. But like all empires that are overgrown and drunk with power, Hollywood will end in infamy, caught between conspiracies, financial crises, and mediocrity.

About the Author

Philosopher and multimedia artist Hervé Fischer graduated from Paris's École Normale Supérieure. He taught sociology of culture and communication for many years at the Sorbonne, and is fluent in French, English, German, and Spanish. He holds a Ph.D. in sociology.

Fischer has worked tirelessly in promoting innovative art forms that utilize science and technology. He is an internationally recognized lecturer and has published numerous articles, papers, and books on art, communications, and digital technologies. One of his most recent works is *Digital Shock*, published by McGill-Queen's University Press in 2006.

Fischer was elected to hold the Daniel Langlois Chair for Fine Arts and Digital Technologies at Concordia University in Montreal (2000–02) and developed the concept of a media lab, a consortium between Concordia and UQAM universities, which has become Hexagram, a non-profit centre of excellence in multimedia research.